Mastering
SEARCH ENGINE OPTIMIZATION
Concepts, Techniques, and Applications

Nikhilesh Mishra,
Author

Website
https://www.nikhileshmishra.com

Copyright Information

i

Dedication

This book is lovingly dedicated to the cherished memory of my father, **Late Krishna Gopal Mishra**, and my mother**, Mrs. Vijay Kanti Mishra.** Their unwavering support, guidance, and love continue to inspire me.

Table of Contents

Author's Preface

Welcome to the captivating world of the knowledge we are about to explore! Within these pages, we invite you to embark on a journey that delves into the frontiers of information and understanding.

Charting the Path to Knowledge

Dive deep into the subjects we are about to explore as we unravel the intricate threads of innovation, creativity, and problem-solving. Whether you're a curious enthusiast, a seasoned professional, or an eager learner, this book serves as your gateway to gaining a deeper understanding.

Your Guiding Light

From the foundational principles of our chosen field to the advanced frontiers of its applications, we've meticulously crafted this book to be your trusted companion. Each chapter is an expedition, guided by expertise and filled with practical insights to empower you on your quest for knowledge.

What Awaits You

- **Illuminate the Origins:** Embark on a journey through the historical evolution of our chosen field, discovering key milestones that have paved the way for breakthroughs.

- **Demystify Complex Concepts:** Grasp the fundamental principles, navigate intricate concepts, and explore practical applications.

- **Mastery of the Craft:** Equip yourself with the skills and knowledge needed to excel in our chosen domain.

Your Journey Begins Here

As we embark on this enlightening journey together, remember that mastery is not just about knowledge but also the wisdom to apply it. Let each chapter be a stepping stone towards unlocking your potential, and let this book be your guide to becoming a true connoisseur of our chosen field.

So, turn the page, delve into the chapters, and immerse yourself in the world of knowledge. Let curiosity be your compass, and let the pursuit of understanding be your guide.

Begin your expedition now. Your quest for mastery awaits!

Sincerely,

Nikhilesh Mishra,

Author

Chapter 1:

Introduction to SEO

Welcome to the exciting world of Search Engine Optimization (SEO), where digital landscapes are shaped, online visibility is earned, and businesses thrive in the digital age. In this chapter, we embark on a journey through the fundamentals of SEO, providing you with a solid foundation upon which to build your expertise. We'll demystify the concept of SEO, explore its historical evolution, and elucidate its profound impact on the ever-evolving digital ecosystem. As we delve into this chapter, prepare to uncover the key principles and essential knowledge that will serve as the bedrock of your SEO mastery. Whether you're a seasoned digital marketer or just taking your first steps into the realm of online optimization, this chapter will set the stage for a comprehensive exploration of the SEO universe.

A. Defining Search Engine Optimization

In the expansive digital universe, where billions of websites vie for attention, Search Engine Optimization (SEO) emerges as the guiding force that determines who rises to the top and who remains hidden in the depths of search engine results pages (SERPs). Understanding what SEO truly means is the first step towards mastering this indispensable art.

What is SEO?

At its core, Search Engine Optimization is a multifaceted discipline aimed at enhancing a website's visibility and ranking on search engine results pages. It involves a strategic and holistic approach to optimizing various aspects of a website, its content, and its online presence to align with the algorithms and criteria used by search engines like Google, Bing, and Yahoo.

The Purpose of SEO

The primary objective of SEO is to connect users with the most relevant and valuable information or services based on their search queries. It accomplishes this by improving a website's chances of appearing prominently in search results when users enter specific keywords or phrases related to the site's content or offerings.

Why is SEO Important?

The significance of SEO in the digital age cannot be overstated. Here's why it matters:

1.   **Enhanced Visibility**: The majority of online experiences begin with a search engine. SEO helps your website be seen by users actively seeking what you offer.

2.   **Credibility and Trust**: Websites ranking higher in search results often enjoy higher levels of trust from users. SEO can help build this trust.

3.   **Cost-Effective Marketing**: Compared to traditional advertising, SEO is cost-effective, providing a sustainable and long-term marketing strategy.

4.   **Competitive Edge**: In a crowded online marketplace, SEO can be your competitive advantage, helping you outrank competitors.

5.   **User Experience**: SEO isn't just about search engines; it's also about improving the user experience on your website, which can lead to higher conversions and customer satisfaction.

The SEO Ecosystem

SEO is a dynamic and ever-evolving field due to constant updates in search engine algorithms and changes in user behavior. It encompasses various components, including:

•   **On-Page Optimization**: Refining the content, structure, and HTML code of web pages to improve search engine relevance.

•   **Off-Page Optimization**: Building a reputable online presence through backlinks, social signals, and other external factors.

- **Technical SEO**: Ensuring that a website's technical infrastructure is search engine-friendly, including aspects like site speed and mobile-friendliness.

- **Local SEO**: Tailoring strategies for local businesses to appear in local search results.

- **Mobile SEO**: Optimizing websites for mobile devices, given the increasing use of smartphones for online activities.

- **Content Strategy**: Creating high-quality, valuable, and relevant content to attract and engage users.

The SEO Journey

The path to mastering SEO is a continuous learning experience. SEO practitioners must stay up-to-date with the latest search engine algorithms, industry trends, and best practices. It involves both the art of understanding user intent and the science of deciphering search engine algorithms.

As we delve deeper into this book, you will gain a comprehensive understanding of these SEO elements and how they work together to propel websites to the forefront of the digital landscape. SEO isn't just about improving rankings; it's about connecting businesses and users, and this chapter serves as your initial step in unraveling the intricacies of this captivating discipline.

B. Historical Evolution of SEO

To truly grasp the complexity and significance of Search Engine Optimization (SEO), it's essential to journey back in time and explore its historical evolution. The story of SEO is one of constant adaptation and innovation in response to the ever-changing digital landscape.

The Early Days: Precursors to SEO

The roots of SEO can be traced back to the early days of the internet when search engines first emerged. In the 1990s, directories like Yahoo and early search engines such as AltaVista and Lycos dominated the online landscape. Webmasters and site owners initially focused on submitting their websites to these directories and optimizing for keywords within their website's meta tags. This rudimentary form of SEO marked the inception of the field.

The Rise of Google: A Game-Changer

The turning point in the history of SEO came with the rise of Google in the late 1990s. Google's innovative PageRank algorithm revolutionized search by ranking websites based on the quality and quantity of links pointing to them. This shift prompted webmasters to focus on link-building strategies to improve their search engine rankings. The concept of backlinks became central to SEO efforts, giving birth to the practice of off-page optimization.

The Era of Keywords: Early 2000s

During the early 2000s, SEO evolved further with a significant emphasis on keyword optimization. This era saw the proliferation of keyword stuffing, a practice in which webmasters would excessively use target keywords in their content, often at the expense of quality and user experience. Search engines, including Google, responded by refining their algorithms to penalize keyword stuffing and prioritize high-quality content.

Content is King: Mid-2000s Onward

As search engines became more sophisticated, they began prioritizing content quality and relevance. Google's algorithm updates, such as the Panda update in 2011, shifted the focus to rewarding websites with valuable, well-structured, and original content while penalizing those with thin or duplicate content. This era marked the ascendancy of content marketing as a core component of SEO.

Mobile Optimization and User Experience: Late 2000s Onward

With the proliferation of smartphones, mobile optimization emerged as a critical SEO consideration. Google's introduction of mobile-first indexing in 2018 underscored the importance of ensuring websites were mobile-friendly. User experience (UX) also gained prominence in SEO, with factors like site speed, accessibility, and responsive design becoming key ranking factors.

The Modern SEO Landscape: Ongoing Evolution

Today, SEO is a multifaceted discipline that continues to evolve. Algorithm updates like Hummingbird, Penguin, and BERT have focused on understanding user intent and providing more relevant search results. Voice search optimization, schema markup for rich snippets, and structured data have become essential elements of modern SEO.

The Future of SEO

The historical evolution of SEO is a testament to its adaptability and resilience. As we look to the future, SEO is poised to remain a vital digital marketing strategy. Emerging technologies like artificial intelligence (AI) and machine learning are expected to play a significant role in shaping SEO by improving search engine algorithms and user experiences.

Understanding this historical context is essential for anyone looking to master SEO. It highlights the field's dynamic nature and underscores the importance of staying informed about industry trends and best practices. As you delve deeper into this book, you'll discover how these historical developments have paved the way for the comprehensive SEO strategies and techniques outlined in subsequent chapters.

C. The Significance of SEO in the Digital Age

In the vast and ever-evolving digital landscape, Search Engine Optimization (SEO) stands as a pillar of digital marketing, a cornerstone that dictates the visibility, reach, and success of businesses and content online. As we explore the significance of SEO in the digital age, we uncover why this practice is not just important but absolutely essential.

1. The Digital Transformation

We live in an era defined by the digital transformation of nearly every aspect of life and business. The internet is the primary conduit through which information is sought, businesses are discovered, and transactions are conducted. In this landscape, search engines serve as the gateways, and SEO is the key to unlock them.

2. The Power of Search Engines

Search engines, led by Google but also including Bing, Yahoo, and others, are the information hubs of the digital age. They process billions of searches every day, connecting users with answers to their questions, solutions to their problems, and products or services they desire. In fact, over 90% of online experiences begin with a search engine. The significance of SEO lies in the fact that it enables your content or business to be discovered in these critical moments of need.

3. Online Visibility and Competitiveness

In a world where thousands of new websites are created every day, online visibility is a fierce battleground. SEO empowers businesses to stand out amidst the digital noise. It helps you rank higher in search results, ensuring that your website is among the first options users encounter. This prominence can make or break your online competitiveness, as users are more likely to click on the top results.

4. Targeted and Qualified Traffic

One of the defining features of SEO is its ability to attract highly targeted and qualified traffic. Unlike some other digital marketing methods, SEO revolves around optimizing for specific keywords or phrases. When users search for these keywords, they are expressing a direct interest in the topic or product, making them more likely to convert into customers or loyal readers.

5. Cost-Effective Marketing

In comparison to traditional advertising methods, SEO offers a cost-effective and sustainable marketing strategy. Paid advertising can quickly deplete budgets, but SEO continues to deliver results over the long term. The investment in optimizing your website and content can provide ongoing returns by driving organic, non-paid traffic.

6. Trust and Credibility

High search engine rankings are often associated with trust and credibility. Users tend to trust the websites that appear at the top of search results. By earning a prominent position, SEO helps establish your brand as a trusted authority in your industry or niche.

7. Adaptation to User Behavior

As user behavior evolves, so does SEO. The digital age has witnessed a shift towards mobile browsing, voice search, and the demand for personalized, location-based results. SEO adapts to these changes, ensuring that your online presence remains aligned with the preferences and habits of your target audience.

8. Data-Driven Decision Making

SEO is not just about optimizing for search engines; it's also about understanding your audience better. SEO tools and analytics provide valuable data and insights about user behavior, preferences, and demographics. This data can inform not only your SEO strategy but also your broader marketing efforts.

In summary, the significance of SEO in the digital age cannot be overstated. It is the linchpin that connects businesses, content creators, and users in a mutually beneficial ecosystem. As we delve deeper into the chapters of this book, you will gain the knowledge and tools necessary to harness the power of SEO and navigate the ever-evolving digital landscape effectively.

D. SEO's Impact on Online Visibility

In the bustling digital realm, where information overload is the norm, online visibility is the lifeblood of success. In this chapter, we dive deep into the profound impact that Search Engine Optimization (SEO) wields over your online presence, and why it's the linchpin for achieving visibility in the crowded online landscape.

1. The Quest for Visibility

Before we explore SEO's impact, let's recognize the fundamental quest for visibility in the digital world. Whether you're running an e-commerce store, publishing content, or offering professional services, your success hinges on being seen by your target audience. Online visibility, therefore, is not merely a luxury but a necessity.

2. The Search Engine Dominance

To appreciate the importance of SEO, we must acknowledge the dominance of search engines, with Google at the forefront. When individuals seek answers, solutions, or products, they turn to search engines. In fact, Google processes over 5.6 billion searches per day. SEO is the compass that guides users to your digital doorstep in this vast online wilderness.

3. Organic vs. Paid Visibility

While paid advertising certainly has its merits, it can be costly and may not always guarantee sustained visibility. Organic visibility, on the other hand, is achieved through the meticulous optimization of your website and content for search engines. This organic approach, which forms the essence of SEO, can drive continuous, long-term traffic to your online assets without the ongoing expense of paid advertising.

4. Ranking Matters

SEO is all about securing top positions in search engine results pages (SERPs). Statistics reveal that the first page of Google receives about 71% of clicks, with the top three results dominating the lion's share. Simply put, the higher you rank, the more visible you are, and the greater your chances of attracting users to your website.

5. Credibility and Trust

SEO isn't just about reaching the top; it's also about building credibility and trust. Websites that consistently appear in top search results are often perceived as authoritative and trustworthy sources of information. SEO can help you earn this coveted position of authority, strengthening your brand's reputation.

6. Targeted Traffic

One of the most compelling aspects of SEO is its ability to attract highly targeted traffic. By optimizing your content for specific keywords and phrases relevant to your niche, you ensure that the users who find your website are actively interested in what you offer. This not only increases the likelihood of conversions but also improves user satisfaction.

7. Global Reach or Local Domination

Whether your goals are global or local, SEO caters to both. For businesses seeking global audiences, SEO can help you compete on an international scale. Conversely, local SEO tactics can position you prominently in local search results, especially crucial for brick-and-mortar businesses.

8. Competitive Edge

In fiercely competitive industries, SEO can be your differentiator. If your competitors are investing in SEO and you're not, you risk falling behind. Conversely, if they are not optimizing their online presence, a well-executed SEO strategy can catapult you ahead.

9. Adapting to User Behavior

The digital landscape is in constant flux, with shifts in user behavior, preferences, and technology. SEO adapts to these changes, ensuring that your online presence remains aligned with the way users search and consume information, whether it's through mobile devices, voice search, or emerging technologies.

In conclusion, SEO's impact on online visibility is pivotal. It is the art and science of ensuring that your digital footprint is not just present but prominent in the online world. As you progress through this book, you'll discover the techniques, strategies, and best practices that will empower you to harness the full potential of SEO, propelling your online visibility to new heights and securing your place in the digital spotlight.

Chapter 2:

Search Engines and Algorithms

In our digital age, where information flows ceaselessly and the internet serves as an infinite reservoir of knowledge and discovery, search engines stand as the gatekeepers to this vast digital universe. To understand how to navigate this realm effectively, we must first unravel the intricate relationship between search engines and the algorithms that power them. In this chapter, we embark on a journey to explore the inner workings of these digital titans, uncovering the pivotal role they play in shaping our online experiences.

The Digital Navigators

Imagine the internet as an immense library, but instead of books, it houses websites, articles, images, videos, and an array of digital content. In this library, search engines are like expert librarians, helping us find the exact information we seek amidst the vast shelves of content. They are the digital navigators, guiding us through the labyrinth of cyberspace.

Search Algorithms: The Secret Sauce

What empowers these digital librarians to deliver the precise results we desire? It's the ingenious concoction of code and logic known as search algorithms. These algorithms are the secret sauce that enables search engines to sift through billions of web pages and rank them in order of relevance when we enter a query.

Understanding the Digital Behavior

To appreciate the intricacies of search engines and algorithms, it's vital to delve into the world of digital behavior. Users enter search queries driven by curiosity, needs, or desires. Search engines, with their algorithms, analyze these queries and crawl the web to fetch pages that best match the user's intent.

The Dynamic Landscape of Search Engines

We'll explore the leading players in the search engine arena, including Google, Bing, Yahoo, and more. Each search engine has its unique algorithms, ranking factors, and approaches to indexing the web. Understanding their differences is crucial for optimizing your online presence effectively.

Algorithm Updates: The Ever-Changing Landscape

Search engine algorithms are not static; they evolve continuously. We'll dive into the realm of algorithm updates, from Google's Panda and Penguin to Hummingbird and beyond. These updates reflect the search engines' commitment to delivering better, more relevant results to users and keeping pace with changing user behaviors and expectations.

Search Engine Behavior and SEO

The significance of understanding search engine behavior extends to Search Engine Optimization (SEO). As you traverse the SEO landscape, you'll realize that it's not merely about optimizing for keywords; it's about aligning your digital presence with the way search engines interpret and respond to user queries. SEO is a symbiotic relationship between your content and search engine algorithms.

The Ongoing Journey

Buckle up as we embark on this voyage of discovery. By the time you navigate the depths of this chapter, you'll be equipped with the knowledge to comprehend the inner workings of search engines and the algorithms that drive them. This understanding is the cornerstone of mastering SEO and harnessing the power of search to make your online presence stand out in the digital realm.

A. Understanding Search Engines (Google, Bing, Yahoo)

In the digital age, search engines are the gatekeepers to a vast repository of information, serving as the digital compass for billions of users worldwide. Understanding the key players in this realm—Google, Bing, and Yahoo—is essential for anyone seeking to master the art of Search Engine Optimization (SEO) and harness the power of online visibility. In this chapter, we delve deep into the inner workings and unique characteristics of these search giants.

Google: The Search Behemoth

Google, with its iconic logo and ubiquitous presence, is synonymous with online search. Founded in 1998, Google's mission is to "organize the world's information and make it universally accessible and useful." Google's dominance in the search engine landscape is nothing short of astounding, with over 90% of global search engine market share.

Key Features of Google:

• **PageRank Algorithm**: Google's PageRank, developed by Larry Page and Sergey Brin, revolutionized search by ranking web pages based on the number and quality of links pointing to them. This algorithm, although evolving, remains at the core of Google's search prowess.

• **User-Centric Approach**: Google places a strong emphasis on providing users with the most relevant, high-quality results. User experience factors, like site speed and mobile-friendliness, have a significant impact on rankings.

• **Algorithm Updates**: Google regularly releases

algorithm updates, with major changes like Panda, Penguin, and BERT aimed at improving search quality and understanding user intent.

Bing: Microsoft's Challenger

Bing, launched by Microsoft in 2009, is a formidable contender in the search engine arena. Although it has a smaller market share than Google, it still holds a significant portion of the search market.

Key Features of Bing:

• **Search Integration**: Bing is deeply integrated with Microsoft products, including Windows, Microsoft Office, and its virtual assistant, Cortana.

• **Visual Search**: Bing has pioneered visual search, allowing users to search using images and even shop for products found in pictures.

• **Unique Ranking Factors**: Bing uses its own set of ranking factors, distinct from Google. Understanding these differences is crucial for effective SEO on Bing.

Yahoo: A Legacy Search Engine

Yahoo, one of the earliest internet giants, has had a storied history in the search realm. While it no longer operates its search technology (having outsourced it to Bing), Yahoo continues to serve as a portal for news, email, and various online services.

Key Features of Yahoo:

- **Content Portal**: Yahoo is known for its homepage, which serves as a content portal featuring news, sports, and entertainment.

- **Yahoo Search Powered by Bing**: In a strategic partnership, Yahoo's search results are powered by Bing, meaning that optimizing for Bing also affects your visibility on Yahoo.

Understanding the Differences

While these search engines share the same fundamental goal—providing users with relevant search results—they each have unique algorithms, ranking factors, and user bases. For SEO practitioners, this means that optimizing for Google may yield different results than optimizing for Bing or Yahoo. Understanding these differences is crucial for tailoring your SEO strategy to target specific search engines or a broader audience.

In conclusion, comprehending the inner workings of Google, Bing, and Yahoo is a pivotal step in mastering SEO. As we navigate further into the intricacies of SEO, you'll gain insights into how to optimize for each of these search engines effectively and adapt to their evolving algorithms. This knowledge will empower you to navigate the diverse and dynamic landscape of online visibility with finesse.

B. The Role of Search Algorithms

In the digital realm, search engines serve as the gateway to the vast expanse of information available on the internet. These search engines rely on complex and ever-evolving algorithms to sift through billions of web pages and deliver relevant results to users. Understanding the pivotal role that search algorithms play in this process is fundamental to mastering the art of Search Engine Optimization (SEO) and achieving online visibility.

1. The Heart of Search Engines

Search algorithms are the beating heart of search engines. They are intricate sets of rules and mathematical formulas designed to determine the order in which web pages appear in search engine results pages (SERPs). These algorithms are responsible for organizing and ranking the vast amount of content available online.

2. Sorting the Digital Universe

Imagine the internet as an immense library with countless books scattered across the shelves. Search algorithms are the librarians who meticulously catalog and index every book, ensuring that when you ask a question or seek information, they can swiftly retrieve the most relevant volumes for you.

3. The Quest for Relevance

At their core, search algorithms are engineered to provide users with the most relevant and valuable results for their queries. They accomplish this by considering a multitude of factors, including keywords, content quality, user engagement, and more.

4. The Evolution of Algorithms

Search algorithms are in a perpetual state of evolution. The digital landscape is dynamic, and user behaviors, technology, and content are constantly changing. Search engines must adapt to these shifts to continue delivering high-quality search results.

5. Major Algorithm Updates

Search engines periodically release significant algorithm updates to improve search quality. These updates can have a profound impact on SEO and online visibility. Some notable algorithm updates include:

- **Panda**: Focused on content quality and penalized low-quality, thin, or duplicate content.

- **Penguin**: Targeted spammy link practices and aimed to promote natural, high-quality link-building.

- **Hummingbird**: Emphasized semantic search, understanding user intent, and delivering more precise results.

- **BERT (Bidirectional Encoder Representations from Transformers)**: A major leap in understanding context and natural language, enhancing the interpretation of complex queries.

6. The User Experience Factor

Modern search algorithms take into account user experience factors, such as site speed, mobile-friendliness, and secure browsing (HTTPS). Search engines aim to provide users with not only relevant content but also a seamless and enjoyable browsing experience.

7. Personalization and Localization

Search algorithms are increasingly personalized, tailoring results to individual user preferences and location. This personalization ensures that users receive content and information that is most relevant to them.

8. User Intent and Context

Understanding user intent is a critical aspect of modern search algorithms. They aim to discern the context of a search query to provide more precise results. For example, a search for "Apple" could refer to the tech company or the fruit, and algorithms aim to differentiate based on context.

9. SEO's Alignment with Algorithms

SEO is intricately connected to search algorithms. Effective SEO strategies involve optimizing content, structure, and user experience in a way that aligns with the factors and criteria that search algorithms consider. SEO practitioners must continually adapt to algorithm updates and industry trends to maintain and improve their online visibility.

In conclusion, search algorithms are the bedrock of search engines and, by extension, the online experience. They are the invisible hands that guide users through the digital maze, connecting them with the information they seek. As we navigate further into the chapters of this book, you'll gain insights into how to optimize your online presence to not only satisfy search algorithms but also provide exceptional value to users, ensuring your place at the forefront of the digital landscape.

C. Algorithm Updates (Panda, Penguin, Hummingbird)

The digital realm is marked by constant evolution, and at the forefront of these changes are search engines like Google, Bing, and Yahoo. To deliver the most relevant and high-quality search results, search engines frequently release algorithm updates. Among the most significant updates in recent history are Google's Panda, Penguin, and Hummingbird algorithms. In this chapter, we explore the profound impact these updates have had on the world of Search Engine Optimization (SEO) and online visibility.

1. Google's Algorithmic Revolution

Google, the search giant, has always been at the forefront of algorithmic innovation. Its core mission is to provide users with the best possible search experience, and to achieve this, Google has introduced numerous algorithm updates over the years.

2. Google Panda: The Content Quality Filter

Launched in February 2011, Google Panda was a game-changer for SEO. It aimed to address the issue of low-quality and thin content that cluttered search results. Key features of Panda include:

• **Content Quality Assessment**: Panda evaluates the quality and relevance of website content. Websites with high-quality, unique, and valuable content were rewarded with higher rankings.

• **Duplicate Content Penalty**: Duplicate content or content that offered little value was penalized, leading to drops in search rankings.

• **User Experience Considerations**: Panda also considered factors like site speed and user engagement, emphasizing a positive user experience.

3. Google Penguin: The Link Quality Enforcer

Released in April 2012, Google Penguin targeted manipulative and spammy link-building practices. Its primary goals were to:

• **Combat Link Spam**: Penguin identified and penalized websites that engaged in tactics like buying links, participating in link farms, or over-optimizing anchor text.

• **Promote Natural Link Building**: The update encouraged websites to focus on earning high-quality, natural backlinks through valuable content and legitimate outreach efforts.

• **Link Quality Assessment**: Penguin assessed the quality of both inbound and outbound links, emphasizing relevance and authority.

4. Google Hummingbird: The Semantic Search Engine

Introduced in August 2013, Google Hummingbird marked a significant leap in the evolution of search algorithms. It aimed to better understand the intent and context behind user queries. Key features of Hummingbird include:

• **Semantic Search**: Hummingbird employed semantic search technology to decipher the meaning and context of search queries, enabling more precise results.

- **Conversational Search**: It allowed Google to better handle conversational queries and voice search, understanding natural language and delivering relevant answers.

- **User Intent Focus**: Hummingbird emphasized understanding user intent, shifting from a purely keyword-based approach to a more holistic understanding of queries.

5. The Impact on SEO and Online Visibility

The introduction of these algorithm updates significantly impacted SEO practices and online visibility:

- **Quality Over Quantity**: Panda and Penguin emphasized the importance of high-quality content and backlinks, shifting the focus from quantity to quality.

- **User-Centric Approach**: Hummingbird underscored the need to align with user intent, encouraging content that addresses user needs and questions.

- **Adaptability**: SEO practitioners had to adapt to the changing landscape, focusing on providing value, a positive user experience, and ethical practices.

In conclusion, the Panda, Penguin, and Hummingbird updates represent pivotal moments in the history of SEO and online visibility. They reflect the ongoing commitment of search engines to deliver the best possible results to users. As you continue your journey through this book, you'll gain insights into how to navigate the ever-evolving world of SEO while aligning with the principles established by these transformative algorithm updates.

D. The Importance of Understanding Search Engine Behavior

In the digital age, where online visibility can make or break businesses and content creators, grasping the intricacies of search engine behavior is paramount. Search engines are the compasses that guide users through the vast digital wilderness. In this chapter, we explore why it's crucial to understand how search engines operate to effectively navigate the terrain of Search Engine Optimization (SEO) and secure your place in the digital spotlight.

1. The Search Engine Ecosystem

Search engines like Google, Bing, and Yahoo are the gateways to the internet. They are the go-to tools for individuals seeking information, products, services, and entertainment. Understanding their behavior is akin to deciphering the rules of engagement in the digital realm.

2. The User-Centric Approach

Search engines are built around user experience. Their primary objective is to provide users with the most relevant, valuable, and trustworthy information in response to their queries. To achieve this, search engines employ complex algorithms that consider various factors when ranking web pages.

3. Keywords and User Intent

At the core of search engine behavior is the relationship between keywords and user intent. Users enter specific words or phrases (keywords) into search engines with the intention of finding information or solutions. Search engines, therefore, analyze these keywords to understand user intent and deliver the most appropriate results.

4. Crawling and Indexing

Search engines use automated bots (spiders or crawlers) to explore the web and gather information from web pages. This process, known as crawling, allows search engines to create an index of web content. Understanding how crawling and indexing work is vital for ensuring that your content is discoverable.

5. Ranking Factors

Search engines employ a multitude of ranking factors to determine the order in which web pages appear in search results. These factors include content quality, relevance, backlinks, user experience, mobile-friendliness, and many more. SEO practitioners must be aware of these factors to optimize their online presence effectively.

6. Algorithm Updates

Search engines regularly release algorithm updates to improve search quality and combat spammy practices. Understanding these updates is critical because they can impact your website's ranking. Staying informed about algorithm changes ensures that your SEO strategy remains current and compliant.

7. Mobile and Voice Search

The rise of mobile devices and voice assistants has transformed search behavior. Search engines have adapted to accommodate mobile-friendly websites and conversational queries. Optimizing for mobile and voice search is essential for reaching today's tech-savvy users.

8. The Evolving Landscape

Search engine behavior is not static; it evolves in response to changes in technology, user behavior, and industry trends. As a result, SEO is an ever-evolving field that requires continuous learning and adaptation.

9. Ethical Considerations

Understanding search engine behavior also encompasses ethical considerations. Search engines reward websites that adhere to ethical SEO practices and penalize those engaged in manipulative tactics. Recognizing the importance of ethical SEO ensures long-term sustainability and trustworthiness.

In conclusion, comprehending search engine behavior is the foundation upon which successful SEO strategies are built. It allows you to align your online presence with the principles and priorities of search engines, ensuring that your content or business stands out in the digital landscape. As you progress through this book, you'll gain valuable insights into how to optimize your digital assets while respecting search engine behavior, ultimately achieving greater online visibility and success.

Chapter 3:

Keyword Research and Analysis

Keywords are the building blocks of online discovery. In this digital age, where search engines are the portals to vast knowledge and solutions, understanding how to harness the power of keywords through comprehensive research and analysis is the key to unlocking online visibility and success. In this chapter, we embark on a journey to unravel the intricacies of keyword research and analysis, a fundamental pillar of effective Search Engine Optimization (SEO) and content strategy.

A. The Fundamentals of Keywords

Keywords are the compass needles that guide users through the digital labyrinth, connecting them with the information, products, and services they seek. Mastering the fundamentals of keywords is foundational to effective Search Engine Optimization (SEO) and content strategy. In this chapter, we delve deep into the core concepts of keywords, understanding their significance, types, and how they serve as the linchpin of online visibility.

1. The Role of Keywords

Keywords are the words or phrases that users type into search engines when seeking information or solutions. They are the bridge between user intent and content relevance. The importance of keywords lies in their ability to connect your content with the needs and queries of your target audience.

2. Types of Keywords

Understanding the different types of keywords is essential for crafting a robust SEO strategy. Here are some common categories:

• **Short-Tail Keywords**: These are brief, often one or two words, and are typically broad in scope (e.g., "shoes" or "travel").

• **Long-Tail Keywords**: Long-tail keywords are longer, more specific phrases (e.g., "running shoes for women with high arches"). They often indicate a higher level of user intent and are less competitive.

• **Branded Keywords**: These include your brand name or variations of it (e.g., "Nike running shoes"). Ranking for your brand terms is essential for brand visibility and reputation management.

• **Transactional Keywords**: These keywords indicate user intent to make a purchase or take action (e.g., "buy iPhone

13" or "subscribe to newsletter").

- **Informational Keywords**: Informational keywords signal that users are seeking knowledge or answers (e.g., "how does photosynthesis work" or "benefits of yoga").

- **Local Keywords**: Local keywords include geographic modifiers (e.g., "pizza near me" or "best dentist in New York"). They are vital for local businesses.

3. Keyword Research Tools

Keyword research begins with selecting the right keywords to target. Several tools and platforms can aid in this process, including:

- **Google Keyword Planner**: Provides keyword suggestions, search volume data, and competition insights.

- **SEMrush**: Offers keyword research, competitive analysis, and tracking capabilities.

- **Ahrefs**: Focuses on backlink analysis but also provides robust keyword research tools.

- **Moz Keyword Explorer**: Offers keyword research and SERP analysis.

4. User Intent

Understanding user intent is crucial for effective keyword selection. User intent refers to the reason behind a search query. Are users looking for information, products, or local services? Are they seeking answers, comparison, or purchase opportunities? Tailoring your keywords to match user intent ensures that your content aligns with what users are looking for.

5. Keyword Volume and Competition

Keyword research tools provide data on search volume (how often a keyword is searched) and competition (how many websites are targeting the keyword). Balancing high-volume keywords with lower competition can be a strategic approach to keyword selection.

6. Content Mapping and Optimization

Once you've identified your target keywords, you can map them to specific pages or content pieces on your website. This process, known as content mapping, helps ensure that each piece of content serves a specific purpose and aligns with user intent.

7. Keyword Trends

Keyword trends can fluctuate over time due to seasonality, events, or shifts in user behavior. Staying informed about keyword trends allows you to adapt your content strategy to remain relevant and timely.

In conclusion, the fundamentals of keywords are the cornerstone of SEO and content strategy. They are the keys that unlock the doors to online visibility and engagement. As you continue your exploration of keyword research and analysis in this chapter, you'll gain the knowledge and tools necessary to harness the power of keywords effectively, ensuring that your digital presence shines brightly in the vast digital landscape.

B. Keyword Research Tools and Techniques

Keyword research is the bedrock of effective Search Engine Optimization (SEO) and content strategy. To unearth the right keywords that will propel your content to the forefront of search engine results, you must employ a combination of tools and techniques. In this chapter, we delve deep into the world of keyword research, exploring the essential tools and techniques that will empower you to uncover the keywords that matter most to your audience.

1. The Art and Science of Keyword Research

Keyword research is both an art and a science. It combines data-driven analysis with creative thinking to identify the words and phrases your target audience uses when searching online. Effective keyword research serves as the foundation upon which you build your content strategy.

2. Keyword Research Tools

A multitude of keyword research tools are available to aid in your quest for the perfect keywords. These tools provide valuable insights into keyword search volume, competition, and related terms. Here are some popular keyword research tools:

- **Google Keyword Planner**: This free tool offers keyword suggestions, search volume data, and competition insights. It's an excellent starting point for beginners.

- **SEMrush**: SEMrush is a comprehensive SEO suite that includes robust keyword research capabilities. It provides not only keyword data but also competitive analysis and tracking.

- **Ahrefs**: While known for its backlink analysis, Ahrefs also offers powerful keyword research tools. It provides data on search volume, keyword difficulty, and more.

- **Moz Keyword Explorer**: Moz's tool offers keyword research and SERP analysis. It provides insights into keyword difficulty and the potential to rank.

- **KeywordTool.io**: This tool specializes in providing keyword suggestions based on Google's autocomplete feature. It's useful for generating long-tail keyword ideas.

3. Techniques for Keyword Research

Effective keyword research involves a systematic approach. Here are some techniques to guide you:

- **Start with Seed Keywords**: Begin with a list of broad, seed keywords related to your niche or topic.

- **Expand with Long-Tail Keywords**: Long-tail keywords are specific phrases that indicate user intent. Expand your list by generating long-tail variations of your seed keywords.

- **Analyze Competitor Keywords**: Investigate the keywords that competitors are targeting. Tools like SEMrush and Ahrefs can provide insights into their keyword strategies.

- **Use Keyword Suggestions**: Keyword research tools often provide keyword suggestions based on user behavior. Explore these suggestions to discover additional relevant keywords.

- **Consider User Intent**: Think about the intent behind each keyword. Are users looking for information, products, or services? Tailor your keywords to match user intent.

- **Evaluate Search Volume and Competition**: Analyze the search volume and competition for each keyword. Balance high-volume keywords with achievable competition levels.

- **Localize Keywords**: If you have a local business, include geographic modifiers in your keywords to target local customers effectively.

- **Regularly Update and Refresh**: Keyword trends can change over time. Periodically revisit your keyword list to ensure it remains up to date and relevant.

4. The Role of Content Mapping

Once you've compiled your list of keywords, map them to specific pages or content pieces on your website. This process, known as content mapping, ensures that each piece of content serves a specific purpose and aligns with user intent.

In conclusion, keyword research is a dynamic and essential aspect of SEO and content strategy. The combination of keyword research tools and techniques empowers you to uncover the keywords that will resonate with your audience and drive organic traffic to your digital assets. As you continue your journey into the world of keyword research, you'll gain the knowledge and skills to make informed keyword choices that will elevate your online visibility and engagement.

C. Long-Tail Keywords and User Intent

In the realm of Search Engine Optimization (SEO), long-tail

keywords and understanding user intent are two vital components that can unlock the full potential of your online visibility and content strategy. In this chapter, we delve deep into the world of long-tail keywords and user intent, exploring how these elements work together to connect your content with the precise needs and queries of your target audience.

1. Long-Tail Keywords: Beyond the Basics

Long-tail keywords are specific phrases, typically consisting of three or more words, that users enter into search engines to find highly targeted information or solutions. They stand in contrast to short-tail keywords, which are shorter and often more generic. Understanding the nuances of long-tail keywords is essential for several reasons:

- **Precise User Intent**: Long-tail keywords are inherently more specific, allowing you to align your content directly with the user's intent. For example, "best running shoes for flat feet" reveals a clear user intent—finding suitable running shoes for a specific condition.

- **Reduced Competition**: Long-tail keywords generally have lower search volumes and, as a result, less competition. This can make it easier to rank for these keywords and capture a niche audience.

- **Higher Conversion Potential**: Users searching with

long-tail keywords often have a well-defined need or problem. This makes them more likely to convert into customers or take desired actions, such as signing up for a newsletter or downloading a resource.

2. The Importance of User Intent

User intent is the underlying motivation behind a user's search query. Understanding user intent is like deciphering the user's language—it helps you provide content that precisely matches what users are looking for. User intent typically falls into several categories:

- **Informational Intent**: Users seek information or answers to questions. For example, "how to tie a tie" or "What is global warming?"

- **Navigational Intent**: Users are looking for a specific website or page. For example, "YouTube" or "Amazon login."

- **Commercial or Transactional Intent**: Users are ready to make a purchase or take a specific action. For example, "buy iPhone 13" or "book a flight to New York."

- **Investigational or Comparison Intent**: Users want to compare options before making a decision. For example, "iPhone vs. Samsung" or "best budget laptop 2023."

- **Local Intent**: Users are searching for products,

services, or information specific to their geographic location. For example, "pizza delivery near me" or "dentist in [city]."

3. Long-Tail Keywords and User Intent Synergy

The synergy between long-tail keywords and user intent is powerful. When you craft content around long-tail keywords that align with user intent, you create a highly focused and relevant user experience. Here's how they work together:

- **Addressing Specific Queries**: Long-tail keywords often mirror specific user queries. By optimizing for these keywords, your content directly addresses user questions or needs.

- **Enhanced User Experience**: Content that caters to user intent provides a superior user experience. It reduces bounce rates and encourages users to engage with your content.

- **Conversion Optimization**: When users find precisely what they're looking for, they are more likely to take desired actions, such as making a purchase or subscribing to your newsletter.

- **Competitive Advantage**: Competing for long-tail keywords with well-matched content can be easier than vying for broad, highly competitive short-tail keywords.

- **Building Authority**: Consistently delivering content that aligns with user intent establishes your website or brand as an authoritative source in your niche.

In conclusion, long-tail keywords and user intent are formidable allies in your quest for online visibility and user engagement. By diving deep into user intent and strategically incorporating long-tail keywords that resonate with your audience's needs, you create a win-win scenario: satisfied users and a strong online presence. As you continue to explore these concepts in this chapter, you'll uncover the strategies and techniques that allow you to harness their power effectively, ensuring your content shines brightly in the digital landscape.

D. Competitor Analysis and Keyword Strategy

In the world of Search Engine Optimization (SEO), staying ahead of the competition is paramount. To achieve this, you must not only understand your competitors but also employ effective keyword strategies that enable you to outmaneuver them. In this chapter, we delve deep into the realms of competitor analysis and keyword strategy, exploring how these components work in tandem to elevate your online visibility and edge ahead in the digital race.

1. Competitor Analysis: The Key to Informed Strategy

Competitor analysis is the process of evaluating the strengths and weaknesses of your competitors in your industry or niche. It's an essential step in shaping your SEO and keyword strategy for several reasons:

- **Identifying Top Competitors**: Understanding who your main competitors are in the digital landscape is crucial. These are the websites or businesses that share your target audience.

- **Gaining Market Insights**: Competitor analysis provides insights into your industry's market dynamics, including trends, user preferences, and potential gaps in content or offerings.

- **Discovering Keywords**: By analyzing competitor websites, you can uncover the keywords they are targeting successfully. This can serve as a valuable source of keyword ideas for your own strategy.

- **Benchmarking Performance**: Comparing your website's performance metrics (e.g., traffic, rankings, conversion rates) to those of competitors allows you to gauge your standing in the industry.

2. Effective Competitor Analysis

To conduct effective competitor analysis, follow these steps:

- **Identify Competitors**: Begin by identifying your primary competitors. These are the websites or businesses that directly compete with you for the same audience.

- **Analyze Their Content**: Examine the types of content your competitors produce. Are they focusing on blog posts, videos, infographics, or other formats? What topics are they covering?

- **Keyword Research**: Investigate the keywords your competitors are targeting. Tools like SEMrush and Ahrefs can provide insights into their keyword strategy.

- **Backlink Analysis**: Analyze your competitors' backlink profiles. Discover which websites are linking to them and identify potential link-building opportunities.

- **User Experience**: Assess the user experience of your competitors' websites. Factors like site speed, mobile-friendliness, and navigation can impact user engagement and SEO rankings.

3. Keyword Strategy: Leveraging Competitor Insights

Keyword strategy is the blueprint that guides your SEO efforts. It's the process of selecting and optimizing keywords to improve your website's visibility in search engine results pages (SERPs). Here's how competitor insights can inform your keyword strategy:

- **Keyword Gap Analysis**: Identify gaps in your keyword strategy compared to your competitors. Are there valuable keywords your competitors are ranking for that you've overlooked?

- **Keyword Prioritization**: Not all keywords are created equal. Prioritize keywords based on factors like search volume, competition, and relevance. Focus on keywords that align with your strengths.

- **Content Strategy**: Develop a content strategy that capitalizes on the keywords your competitors are targeting. Create high-quality, in-depth content that addresses user needs better than your competitors.

- **Long-Tail Keywords**: Explore long-tail keywords that competitors may have overlooked. These can be a source of niche traffic and lower competition.

- **Local SEO**: If your business serves a local market, pay attention to competitor strategies for local SEO. Optimize your website for local keywords and Google My Business to compete effectively.

4. Staying Ahead: Continuous Monitoring

Competitor analysis and keyword strategy are not one-time exercises; they require continuous monitoring and adaptation. The digital landscape is dynamic, and your competitors' tactics may evolve. To stay ahead:

- **Regularly Update Keywords**: Periodically revisit your keyword strategy to identify emerging trends and shifting competitor strategies.

• **Track Performance**: Monitor the performance of your keywords and content compared to competitors. Adjust your strategy based on performance metrics.

• **Innovate and Differentiate**: Seek opportunities to innovate and differentiate your offerings and content from competitors. Standing out can give you a competitive edge.

In conclusion, competitor analysis and keyword strategy are indispensable tools for achieving and maintaining online visibility and success. By dissecting your competition and leveraging their insights, you can formulate a keyword strategy that positions you as a formidable player in the digital arena. As you proceed with this chapter, you'll uncover the techniques and tactics that will enable you to not only keep pace with your competitors but also surpass them in the ever-evolving world of SEO.

E. Keyword Mapping and On-Page Optimization

Once you've conducted comprehensive keyword research and competitor analysis, the next critical steps in your Search Engine Optimization (SEO) journey are keyword mapping and on-page optimization. In this chapter, we'll delve deep into these essential practices, exploring how they work in tandem to fine-tune your content and ensure it aligns perfectly with the keywords you want to target.

1. Keyword Mapping: The Blueprint of Your Content Strategy

Keyword mapping is the process of assigning specific keywords or keyword groups to individual pages or pieces of content on your website. Think of it as creating a strategic blueprint that ensures your content is laser-focused on particular keywords. Here's why keyword mapping is crucial:

- **Content Relevance**: Mapping keywords to specific pages ensures that your content is highly relevant to the targeted keywords. This improves the user experience and SEO.

- **Efficient Optimization**: It streamlines the optimization process. You can tailor each page's content, meta tags, and other elements to the keywords it's mapped to.

- **Avoiding Keyword Cannibalization**: Keyword cannibalization occurs when multiple pages on your site compete for the same keyword. Keyword mapping helps prevent this issue.

2. Steps for Effective Keyword Mapping

To create an effective keyword map, follow these steps:

- **Group Keywords**: Group related keywords together

based on topics or user intent. For example, group keywords related to "running shoes" together.

- **Assign Keywords to Pages**: Match these keyword groups with specific pages or content pieces on your site. Ensure that the content on each page aligns with the assigned keywords.

- **Prioritize Keywords**: Consider the importance and competitiveness of keywords when assigning them to pages. High-value keywords may be best suited to your core landing pages.

- **Create a Visual Map**: Many SEO professionals use visual diagrams or spreadsheets to map keywords to pages. This helps visualize the structure of your website's content.

3. On-Page Optimization: Refining Your Content for SEO

On-page optimization is the process of fine-tuning individual web pages to improve their search engine rankings and user experience. It encompasses various elements, including content, meta tags, headers, and more. Effective on-page optimization ensures that your content not only ranks well but also engages and satisfies users. Here are key components of on-page optimization:

- **Title Tags**: Craft descriptive and keyword-rich title tags for each page. These tags appear as the clickable headlines in search engine results.

- **Meta Descriptions**: Write compelling meta descriptions that summarize the page's content and include relevant keywords. While not a direct ranking factor, meta descriptions impact click-through rates.

- **Header Tags**: Use header tags (H1, H2, H3, etc.) to structure your content logically. Include keywords in headers to signal the topic to search engines.

- **Content Optimization**: Ensure that your content is high-quality, relevant, and comprehensive. Incorporate keywords naturally but avoid keyword stuffing. Focus on providing value to the reader.

- **Image SEO**: Optimize images by using descriptive file names and alt text. This not only improves accessibility but also contributes to SEO.

- **URL Structure**: Create clean and descriptive URLs that include relevant keywords. Avoid long, complex URLs with unnecessary parameters.

- **Internal Linking**: Include internal links to relevant pages within your content. This helps search engines crawl your site and provides a better user experience.

- **Mobile-Friendly Design**: Ensure that your pages are responsive and mobile-friendly. Mobile optimization is crucial for

SEO and user satisfaction.

- **Page Speed**: Improve page load times for a better user experience. Faster-loading pages tend to rank higher in search results.

4. The User-Centric Approach

While on-page optimization is vital for SEO, it's equally important to keep the user in mind. Prioritize user experience, readability, and engagement when optimizing your content. SEO success often goes hand in hand with providing valuable and satisfying experiences for your audience.

In conclusion, keyword mapping and on-page optimization are integral components of an effective SEO strategy. By meticulously mapping keywords to specific pages and optimizing those pages with user experience in mind, you create a harmonious balance that not only boosts your search engine rankings but also enhances the overall quality of your content. As you continue to explore these practices in this chapter, you'll gain the knowledge and techniques necessary to optimize your digital assets for maximum visibility and user engagement.

Chapter 4:

On-Page SEO

On-page SEO is the art and science of optimizing individual web pages to rank higher in search engine results and provide a superior user experience. In this chapter, we delve deep into the realm of on-page SEO, exploring the techniques and strategies that will empower you to fine-tune your web content, making it not only more appealing to search engines but also more valuable to your audience. From title tags to content quality, we'll cover the essentials of on-page optimization.

A. Title Tags, Meta Descriptions, and Headers in On-Page SEO

Title tags, meta descriptions, and headers are fundamental elements of on-page SEO that play a pivotal role in optimizing web pages for both search engines and users. In this chapter, we'll explore these critical components in depth, understanding how they impact search engine rankings, user experience, and the overall success of your digital content strategy.

1. Title Tags: The Gateway to Your Content

Title tags are the clickable headlines that appear in search engine results and browser tabs when users visit your webpage. They are the first impression users have of your content and serve as a critical ranking factor. Here's why title tags matter:

- **SEO Significance**: Search engines give considerable weight to title tags when determining a page's topic and relevance to search queries. Including target keywords in your title tags can improve your ranking for those keywords.

- **User Click-Through Rates**: A well-crafted title tag can entice users to click on your link in search results. It should be descriptive, compelling, and accurately represent the page's content.

- **Branding**: Title tags often include your brand name, helping users recognize your site and fostering trust.

- **Browser Tab Identification**: When users have multiple tabs open in their browser, the title tag helps them quickly identify your page.

2. Meta Descriptions: The Content Preview

Meta descriptions are short, concise summaries of a webpage's content. While not a direct ranking factor, they serve several crucial purposes:

- **User Engagement**: An engaging meta description can persuade users to click on your link in search results, improving click-through rates (CTR).

- **Content Preview**: Meta descriptions provide a sneak peek into what users can expect to find on your page, helping them make informed choices about which results to click on.

- **Keyword Presence**: Including relevant keywords in your meta description can reinforce the page's relevance to search queries.

3. Headers: Structuring Your Content

Headers, designated using HTML tags such as H1, H2, H3, and so on, help structure your content and make it more accessible to both users and search engines. Here's how headers contribute to on-page SEO:

- **Hierarchy and Organization**: Headers establish a hierarchy within your content, with H1 typically denoting the main heading or title of the page, followed by subheadings (H2, H3, etc.). This hierarchy helps search engines understand the structure and importance of content sections.

- **Keyword Emphasis**: Including keywords in headers signals their importance to search engines. It can also improve the readability and scannability of your content for users.

- **User Experience**: Headers break up long blocks of text, making your content more visually appealing and easier to navigate for users.

4. Best Practices for Title Tags, Meta Descriptions, and Headers

To maximize the effectiveness of these elements, follow these best practices:

- **Title Tags**:

- Keep them concise, typically under 60 characters to ensure they display fully in search results.

- Include the primary keyword near the beginning of the title.

- Craft unique titles for each page on your website.

- Create compelling titles that encourage clicks while accurately representing your content.

- **Meta Descriptions**:

- Limit them to around 160 characters for optimal display.

- Make them informative and persuasive.

- Avoid duplicate meta descriptions across pages.

- Include relevant keywords naturally.

- **Headers**:

- Use a clear hierarchy with H1 for the main title, followed by H2 for subsections, and so on.

- Include keywords in headers where appropriate, but prioritize readability and user experience.

- Keep headers concise and descriptive.

In conclusion, title tags, meta descriptions, and headers are indispensable components of on-page SEO that directly impact your website's search engine rankings and user engagement. By optimizing these elements thoughtfully, you can not only improve your search visibility but also provide a more enjoyable and informative experience for your audience. As you delve deeper into on-page SEO in this chapter, you'll gain the insights and techniques necessary to master these critical elements and enhance the overall effectiveness of your digital content.

B. Content Optimization (Quality, Relevance, Length) in On-Page SEO

Content is at the heart of your website's ability to rank well in search engines and provide value to your audience. In this chapter, we explore the multifaceted world of content optimization in on-page SEO, emphasizing the importance of quality, relevance, and length in crafting content that not only pleases search engines but also engages and satisfies your users.

1. Quality Content: The Cornerstone of SEO

Quality content is the foundation upon which your on-page SEO efforts stand. It encompasses several key aspects:

- **Accuracy and Authority**: Your content should be accurate, well-researched, and authoritative in its field. Cite reliable sources and provide evidence where necessary.

- **Uniqueness**: Avoid duplicate content. Each page should offer unique, valuable information to users.

- **Engagement**: Engaging content captures and retains users' attention. Use storytelling, visuals, and multimedia elements to make your content more compelling.

- **Readability**: Content should be easy to read and understand. Use clear language, concise sentences, and well-structured paragraphs.

- **Relevance**: Ensure that your content is relevant to the topic or keywords you're targeting. Avoid off-topic tangents that could confuse both users and search engines.

- **User Intent**: Address user intent effectively.

Understand what users are looking for when searching for specific keywords and tailor your content to meet those needs.

2. Relevance to User Queries and Intent

Relevance is a critical factor in on-page SEO. To create relevant content:

- **Keyword Integration**: Incorporate target keywords naturally within your content. However, avoid keyword stuffing, which can harm your rankings.

- **Semantic Keywords**: Include semantically related keywords and phrases. Search engines use semantic analysis to understand the context of content.

- **User-Centric Approach**: Focus on addressing user queries and needs. Your content should provide valuable information or solutions that match user intent.

- **Topic Clusters**: Consider creating content clusters around a central topic. This helps establish your authority on the subject and can improve rankings.

3. Content Length: Striking the Right Balance

Content length is a topic of debate in SEO. While there's no one-size-fits-all answer, here are considerations to help you strike the right balance:

- **Comprehensive Coverage**: Some topics require in-depth coverage to satisfy user intent. Longer content may be necessary for comprehensive guides or tutorials.

- **User Attention Span**: Consider user attention spans. For some queries, shorter, concise content may be more suitable and engaging.

- **Competitor Analysis**: Analyze the content length of top-ranking pages for your target keywords. This can provide insights into user expectations.

- **Quality Over Quantity**: Always prioritize content quality over length. Long-form content should maintain user engagement and provide value throughout.

4. Optimizing Multimedia Content

Multimedia elements like images, videos, infographics, and interactive content can enhance your on-page SEO efforts:

- **Image SEO**: Optimize images by using descriptive file names, alt text, and captions. This improves accessibility and can lead to image search traffic.

- **Video Optimization**: If you embed videos, ensure they are relevant to your content. Include video titles, descriptions, and transcripts for SEO.

- **Interactive Content**: Interactive content such as quizzes, calculators, and surveys can boost user engagement and time spent on your page.

5. The Role of User Experience (UX)

User experience is closely tied to content optimization. A seamless, enjoyable user experience can lead to higher rankings and user satisfaction:

- **Page Load Speed**: Ensure your content loads quickly to prevent user frustration and high bounce rates.

- **Mobile Optimization**: Make your content responsive and mobile-friendly to accommodate users on various devices.

- **Navigation**: Easy navigation helps users find relevant content. Use internal links and clear menus to guide users.

In conclusion, content optimization is a multifaceted practice that involves balancing quality, relevance, and length to meet the needs of both users and search engines. By creating content that engages, informs, and satisfies user intent while adhering to SEO best practices, you can improve your website's rankings and provide a valuable online experience. As you explore the nuances of content optimization in this chapter, you'll gain the knowledge and techniques necessary to craft content that excels in the competitive digital landscape.

C. Image SEO and Alt Text in On-Page SEO

Images are a powerful visual component of web content, enhancing user engagement and understanding. However, for search engines to interpret and rank images effectively, image SEO and the use of alt text are essential. In this chapter, we'll dive deep into the world of image optimization and alt text, uncovering their significance, best practices, and impact on your on-page SEO efforts.

1. The Importance of Image SEO

Image SEO, also known as image optimization, refers to the process of enhancing the visibility and accessibility of images on your website. Proper image SEO is essential for several reasons:

- **Improved User Experience**: High-quality images enhance user engagement and understanding of your content, making it more appealing.

- **Faster Loading Times**: Optimized images contribute to faster page load times, which is a ranking factor in SEO.

- **Enhanced Accessibility**: Proper image SEO, including alt text, makes your content accessible to users with disabilities who rely on screen readers.

- **Potential for Image Search Traffic**: Optimized images can appear in image search results, driving additional organic traffic to your website.

2. Alt Text: The Eyes of Search Engines

Alt text, short for "alternative text," is a concise description of an image's content. It serves as a textual representation of the image and plays a crucial role in both SEO and accessibility. Here's why alt text is essential:

- **SEO Value**: Search engines use alt text to understand and index images. Including relevant keywords in alt text can improve your image's chances of ranking in image search results.

- **Accessibility**: Alt text is crucial for users with visual impairments who rely on screen readers. It provides a description of the image's content, ensuring that everyone can access and understand your content.

- **Display in Case of Image Failure**: If an image fails to load for any reason, the alt text is displayed in its place, ensuring users still receive context and information.

3. Best Practices for Alt Text

Crafting effective alt text requires a balance between clarity, conciseness, and relevance. Here are some best practices to follow:

- **Be Descriptive**: Describe the image's content

accurately and concisely. Use clear, plain language.

• **Include Relevant Keywords**: If applicable, incorporate relevant keywords in your alt text, but do so naturally and without keyword stuffing.

• **Keep It Concise**: Alt text should be brief but comprehensive. Aim for a sentence or a few words that capture the image's essence.

• **Avoid "Image of" or "Picture of"**: There's no need to start alt text with "image of" or similar phrases. Focus on the content itself.

• **Omit Decorative Images**: If an image is purely decorative and doesn't convey meaningful content, it's acceptable to use empty alt text (alt=""). This tells screen readers to ignore the image.

4. Image Optimization Techniques

In addition to alt text, consider the following image optimization techniques:

• **File Compression**: Compress image files to reduce their size without sacrificing quality. Smaller file sizes lead to faster page load times.

• **File Format**: Choose the appropriate file format for

your images. JPEG is suitable for photographs, while PNG is better for images with transparency.

- **Image Dimensions**: Specify the image dimensions in your HTML code. This prevents the page from reflowing as images load and improves user experience.

- **Image Sitemaps**: Submit an image sitemap to search engines to ensure that they index your images effectively.

5. User Experience and Image Placement

In addition to image optimization, consider the user experience when placing images on your web pages:

- **Relevance**: Ensure that images are relevant to the surrounding content and support the user's understanding of the topic.

- **Placement**: Position images strategically within your content to break up text, illustrate points, and maintain visual interest.

- **Captioning**: If appropriate, provide captions for images. Captions can enhance user engagement and clarify image context.

In conclusion, image SEO and alt text are vital components of on-page SEO that enhance the accessibility, user experience, and search engine visibility of your web content. By optimizing your images, crafting descriptive alt text, and considering the user experience, you can create a visually compelling and SEO-friendly online presence. As you continue to explore image SEO and alt text in this chapter, you'll gain the knowledge and skills necessary to make your web content visually appealing and accessible to all users.

D. URL Structure and Internal Linking in On-Page SEO

URL structure and internal linking are two interconnected aspects of on-page SEO that profoundly influence your website's search engine rankings, user experience, and overall navigation. In this chapter, we'll delve deep into the world of URL optimization and internal linking, exploring their significance, best practices, and how they contribute to a well-structured and search-friendly website.

1. URL Structure: The Roadmap to Your Content

URLs (Uniform Resource Locators) serve as the digital addresses for your web pages. They not only provide a path to your content but also offer valuable clues to search engines and users about what the page contains. Here's why URL structure matters:

- **SEO Significance**: Search engines analyze URLs to determine the topic and relevance of a page. A well-structured URL with relevant keywords can positively impact your rankings.

- **User-Friendly Navigation**: Clear and descriptive URLs make it easier for users to understand the content of a page and navigate your website.

- **Shareability**: Readable URLs are more likely to be shared on social media and linked to by other websites.

2. Best Practices for URL Structure

To optimize your URL structure for SEO and user experience, consider the following best practices:

- **Descriptive and Readable**: Create URLs that are descriptive and readable to both humans and search engines. Avoid cryptic or excessively long strings of characters.

- **Include Keywords**: Include relevant keywords in your URLs, but do so naturally. Keywords should accurately reflect the content of the page.

- **Hyphens for Separation**: Use hyphens (-) to separate words in URLs rather than underscores (_) or spaces. Hyphens are recognized as word separators by search engines.

- **Avoid Special Characters**: Minimize the use of

special characters, symbols, or query parameters in your URLs. These can complicate readability and indexing.

• **Keep It Short**: Aim for concise URLs. While there's no strict character limit, shorter URLs are generally more user-friendly and easier to share.

3. Internal Linking: The Digital Pathways

Internal linking is the practice of creating hyperlinks within your content that point to other pages on your website. These links serve as digital pathways, guiding users and search engine crawlers through your site's content. Internal linking is essential for several reasons:

• **Navigation**: It enhances website navigation, allowing users to easily move between related pages.

• **Distributing Link Equity**: Internal links distribute link equity (or "link juice") throughout your website, helping all pages, including new ones, potentially rank higher.

• **Content Relevance**: Internal links establish relationships between related pieces of content, signaling to search engines which pages are important and relevant.

• **Indexing**: Search engine crawlers use internal links to discover and index new content on your website.

4. Best Practices for Internal Linking

To maximize the benefits of internal linking, follow these best practices:

- **Use Descriptive Anchor Text**: The text you use for internal links (anchor text) should be descriptive and provide context about the linked page's content.

- **Link to Relevant Pages**: Ensure that the pages you link to are genuinely relevant to the content of the source page.

- **Limit the Number of Links**: Avoid overloading pages with excessive internal links, as this can overwhelm users and dilute the significance of each link.

- **Deep Linking**: Don't just link to your homepage. Deep-link to specific, relevant pages within your website.

- **Regularly Audit Links**: Periodically review your internal links to ensure they remain functional and relevant.

5. User Experience and Site Structure

The user experience is closely tied to URL structure and internal linking. A well-structured site with intuitive navigation enhances the user experience:

- **Logical Hierarchy**: Organize your content into a logical hierarchy, with clear categories and subcategories. This makes it easier for users to find what they're looking for.

• **Breadcrumbs**: Implement breadcrumbs on your site to show users their current location within your site's structure. Breadcrumbs aid navigation and provide context.

• **Sitemap**: Include an HTML sitemap page that lists all major sections and pages on your site. This can serve as a valuable navigational tool.

In conclusion, URL structure and internal linking are foundational elements of on-page SEO that impact how search engines and users discover and navigate your website. By optimizing your URL structure for readability and including relevant keywords, and by implementing a well-thought-out internal linking strategy, you can create a more user-friendly, search-engine-friendly, and organized website. As you continue to explore these practices in this chapter, you'll gain the knowledge and skills necessary to structure your website effectively and enhance both user experience and search engine visibility.

E. Mobile-Friendly and Responsive Design in On-Page SEO

Mobile-friendly and responsive design are integral components of on-page SEO in today's digital landscape, where a significant portion of web traffic comes from mobile devices. In this chapter, we will explore the importance of mobile optimization, the principles of responsive design, and best practices for ensuring your website delivers an exceptional user experience across all screen sizes.

1. The Significance of Mobile Optimization

Mobile optimization refers to the process of ensuring that your website and its content are accessible, visually appealing, and fully functional on mobile devices such as smartphones and tablets. Mobile optimization is vital for several reasons:

- **Mobile Usage**: With the widespread use of smartphones, a significant portion of internet traffic comes from mobile devices. Ignoring mobile optimization can lead to a poor user experience for a substantial portion of your audience.

- **Google's Mobile-First Indexing**: Google prioritizes mobile-friendly websites in its rankings. In 2018, Google switched to mobile-first indexing, which means it primarily uses the mobile version of your site for ranking and indexing.

- **User Experience**: A mobile-friendly website provides an improved user experience, reducing bounce rates and encouraging longer visit durations.

- **Competitive Advantage**: Mobile optimization can give you a competitive advantage in search rankings and user satisfaction compared to websites that are not mobile-friendly.

2. Principles of Responsive Design

Responsive web design is a design approach that ensures your website's layout and content adapt fluidly to various screen sizes and devices. Here are key principles of responsive design:

- **Fluid Grids**: Use relative units like percentages rather than fixed units like pixels for layout elements. This allows content to resize smoothly across screens.

- **Flexible Images and Media**: Use CSS to ensure that images and media scale proportionally to fit different screen sizes without distortion.

- **Media Queries**: Employ media queries in your CSS to apply specific styles and layouts based on screen width, height, and device orientation. This allows for targeted adjustments.

- **Mobile-First Approach**: Start designing and building your website with a mobile-first mentality. This ensures that the mobile experience is prioritized and later enhanced for larger screens.

3. Best Practices for Mobile-Friendly Design

To create a mobile-friendly website that excels in on-page SEO and user satisfaction, consider the following best practices:

- **Responsive Design**: Implement a responsive design framework that adapts your website's layout and content seamlessly to various screen sizes.

- **Optimize Images**: Compress and optimize images for fast loading on mobile devices. Use responsive image techniques to serve appropriate image sizes based on device capabilities.

- **Clear and Tappable Elements**: Ensure that buttons, links, and interactive elements are appropriately sized and spaced for touch interaction. Aim for a minimum tap target size of 48x48 pixels.

- **Readable Text**: Use legible font sizes and styles that are easy to read on smaller screens. Avoid small text that requires pinch-zooming.

- **Fast Loading**: Minimize unnecessary scripts, plugins, and other resources that can slow down your website's loading speed on mobile devices.

- **Mobile SEO**: Pay attention to mobile-specific SEO elements, such as mobile-friendly tags in your HTML, to signal to search engines that your site is optimized for mobile.

- **Test Across Devices**: Regularly test your website across various mobile devices and browsers to ensure consistent performance and appearance.

- **Mobile-Friendly Testing Tools**: Use Google's Mobile-Friendly Test and other mobile optimization tools to evaluate your website's mobile-friendliness.

4. User Experience and Mobile Optimization

Mobile optimization goes beyond technical considerations; it is also about providing an excellent user experience. Prioritize the following aspects for a seamless mobile experience:

- **Navigation**: Simplify navigation menus for mobile users, using collapsible menus or icons to conserve screen space.

- **Loading Speed**: Optimize loading times to ensure quick access to content on mobile devices, even on slower connections.

- **Content Prioritization**: Prioritize and present the most critical content and calls to action prominently on mobile screens.

- **Forms and Checkout**: Streamline form fields and the checkout process to minimize friction and user input on mobile devices.

In conclusion, mobile-friendly and responsive design are indispensable for on-page SEO and user satisfaction in the mobile-centric digital era. By adhering to the principles of responsive design, implementing best practices for mobile optimization, and considering the mobile user experience, you can ensure that your website not only ranks well in mobile search results but also provides a seamless and enjoyable experience for all visitors, regardless of the device they use. As you continue to explore these practices in this chapter, you'll gain the knowledge and skills necessary to create a mobile-friendly and responsive website that excels in the competitive online landscape.

Chapter 5:

Off-Page SEO

Off-page SEO is the art and science of optimizing your online presence beyond your website to improve its visibility and authority in the digital world. In this chapter, we embark on a journey into the realm of off-page SEO, where we explore the strategies and tactics that extend your influence, reputation, and relevance throughout the vast landscape of the internet. From building quality backlinks to managing your online reputation, we uncover the intricacies of off-page SEO and its pivotal role in boosting your website's performance.

A. Backlinks and Link Building Strategies in Off-Page SEO

Backlinks and link building are foundational elements of off-page SEO that play a pivotal role in your website's authority, visibility, and search engine rankings. In this chapter, we delve deep into the world of backlinks and explore effective link building strategies, understanding their significance and the best practices that can propel your website to the forefront of search engine results.

1. The Significance of Backlinks

Backlinks, also known as inbound links or incoming links, are hyperlinks from other websites to your own. They serve as digital endorsements and references, signaling to search engines that your content is valuable, credible, and worth ranking. Here's why backlinks are crucial:

- **Authority and Trust**: Search engines view backlinks as votes of confidence. When reputable websites link to your content, it boosts your website's authority and trustworthiness in the eyes of search engines.

- **Traffic Generation**: High-quality backlinks can drive direct referral traffic to your website. Users click on these links to explore related content, potentially becoming loyal visitors.

- **Improved Rankings**: Backlinks are a significant ranking factor in search engine algorithms. Websites with a strong backlink profile tend to rank higher for relevant keywords.

2. Link Building Strategies

Effective link building involves strategically acquiring backlinks from reputable sources. Here are proven link building strategies to bolster your off-page SEO efforts:

a. High-Quality Content Creation

Quality content is a magnet for natural backlinks. When you produce valuable, informative, and unique content, other websites are more likely to link to it organically. Strategies include:

- **Comprehensive Guides**: Craft in-depth guides, tutorials, or resources that become go-to references in your industry.

- **Original Research**: Conduct and publish original research, surveys, or studies that others can reference.

- **Infographics and Visual Content**: Create visually appealing content like infographics that are highly shareable.

b. Guest Blogging

Guest blogging involves writing content for other websites in your niche. In exchange for your expertise, you receive a backlink to your website. Key considerations include:

- **Relevant Websites**: Target websites that are closely related to your industry or niche.

- **Quality Content**: Ensure that your guest posts provide real value to readers and align with the host site's content.

- **Author Bio**: Include a well-crafted author bio that introduces you and links back to your website.

c. Broken Link Building

This strategy involves finding broken (non-working) links on other websites and reaching out to suggest replacing them with a link to your relevant content. It's a win-win approach for both parties:

- **Prospecting**: Identify websites in your niche with broken links using tools like Check My Links or Broken Link Checker.

- **Outreach**: Contact the site owner or webmaster, politely pointing out the broken link and suggesting your content as a replacement.

d. Outreach and Relationship Building

Build relationships with influencers, industry leaders, and webmasters in your niche. This can lead to natural link opportunities when these connections find your content valuable:

- **Social Media Engagement**: Connect on social platforms, share each other's content, and foster genuine relationships.

- **Email Outreach**: Reach out with personalized, non-spammy emails to introduce yourself and your content.

e. Content Syndication and Repurposing

Syndicate your content on reputable platforms like Medium or LinkedIn. While these platforms may use canonical tags to avoid duplicate content issues, they can still drive traffic and indirect backlinks.

- **Repurposing**: Transform existing content into different formats like podcasts, videos, or ebooks. Promote these formats on relevant platforms for broader exposure.

3. Assessing Backlink Quality

Not all backlinks are created equal. To ensure your link building efforts are effective, focus on quality rather than quantity:

- **Relevance**: Backlinks from websites related to your niche or industry carry more weight.

- **Authority**: Aim for backlinks from authoritative websites with high domain authority (DA) and PageRank.

- **Diversity**: A diverse backlink profile includes a variety of sources, such as blogs, news sites, forums, and social media.

- **Natural vs. Manipulated**: Google values naturally acquired backlinks over those obtained through manipulative tactics like link farms or excessive link exchanges.

4. Monitoring and Maintaining Your Backlink Profile

Regularly monitor your backlink profile to ensure its health and quality. Use tools like Google Search Console, Ahrefs, or Moz to:

- **Identify New Backlinks**: Stay aware of new websites linking to your content.

- **Check for Toxic Backlinks**: Identify and disavow toxic or spammy backlinks that could harm your site's reputation.

- **Track Lost Backlinks**: Monitor for lost or broken backlinks and address them when necessary.

In conclusion, backlinks and link building strategies are cornerstones of off-page SEO that directly impact your website's authority and search engine rankings. By creating valuable content, engaging in guest blogging, and building relationships within your industry, you can develop a robust backlink profile that boosts your online presence and drives organic traffic. As you continue to explore these strategies in this chapter, you'll gain the knowledge and skills necessary to establish a formidable backlink profile and elevate your website's visibility in the competitive digital landscape.

B. Social Media Signals and SEO in Off-Page SEO

In the ever-evolving landscape of off-page SEO, social media signals have emerged as a dynamic and influential factor that can significantly impact your website's visibility, authority, and overall search engine optimization efforts. In this chapter, we'll delve deep into the synergy between social media and SEO, uncovering the importance of social signals and how to leverage them to enhance your online presence.

1. Understanding Social Media Signals

Social media signals encompass various interactions and activities related to your content on social media platforms. These signals indicate how users engage with your content, and they can have a profound impact on your SEO efforts. Key social media signals include:

• **Likes and Shares**: The number of likes and shares your content receives reflects its popularity and reach on social media.

• **Comments and Engagement**: Meaningful conversations and interactions in the form of comments, replies, and discussions can signal content relevance and quality.

• **Followers and Subscribers**: The size and growth of your social media following can demonstrate your brand's influence and authority in your niche.

- **Click-Through Rates (CTR)**: The rate at which users click on links to your website shared on social media platforms can influence search engine rankings.

2. The Impact of Social Media Signals on SEO

Social media signals can indirectly impact your website's SEO in several ways:

- **Increased Website Traffic**: When your content gains traction on social media, it can drive more users to your website. Increased traffic can boost your search engine rankings.

- **Brand Visibility**: Social media provides a platform for increasing brand visibility and recognition, which can lead to branded searches and improved SEO.

- **Backlinks**: Social media shares can result in backlinks from other websites, contributing to your backlink profile's diversity and quality.

- **Content Indexing**: Social media platforms are frequently crawled by search engines. Sharing your content on these platforms can lead to quicker indexing by search engine bots.

- **User Engagement**: High levels of social engagement

can signal content quality to search engines, potentially improving rankings.

3. Leveraging Social Media for SEO

To harness the power of social media signals for SEO, follow these strategies:

• **Content Promotion**: Share your high-quality content on social media platforms to increase its visibility and encourage engagement.

• **Engagement and Interaction**: Actively engage with your audience on social media. Respond to comments, answer questions, and foster discussions around your content.

• **Social Sharing Buttons**: Incorporate social sharing buttons on your website to make it easy for users to share your content on their social profiles.

• **Content Optimization**: Craft social media posts with compelling headlines, descriptions, and visuals to entice users to click through to your website.

• **Consistency**: Maintain an active and consistent social media presence to keep your audience engaged and informed.

4. Social Media Platforms and SEO

Different social media platforms offer unique opportunities for

SEO. Here's a brief overview of how some popular platforms can impact your SEO efforts:

- **Facebook**: Sharing content and engaging with your audience on Facebook can enhance brand visibility and drive traffic to your website.

- **Twitter**: Twitter is a real-time platform where timely tweets can generate immediate engagement and traffic to your site.

- **LinkedIn**: LinkedIn is ideal for B2B businesses. Sharing thought leadership content and building connections can lead to industry authority and backlinks.

- **Instagram**: Visual content on Instagram can attract a younger demographic and encourage users to explore your website.

- **Pinterest**: Visual content shared on Pinterest can drive traffic to your site, particularly if you're in the e-commerce or DIY niche.

- **YouTube**: YouTube is the second-largest search engine globally, making it a valuable platform for SEO through video content.

5. Measuring Social Media Impact

To assess the impact of social media signals on your SEO

efforts, monitor and analyze metrics like website traffic, social engagement, follower growth, and backlinks. Tools like Google Analytics, social media analytics dashboards, and SEO software can provide valuable insights into your social media performance and its correlation with SEO outcomes.

In conclusion, social media signals are an integral part of off-page SEO that can significantly influence your website's visibility and authority in search engine rankings. By actively engaging with your audience, promoting your content, and leveraging the unique opportunities offered by different social media platforms, you can amplify the impact of social media on your SEO efforts. As you explore these strategies in this chapter, you'll gain the knowledge and skills necessary to harness the synergy between social media and SEO, ultimately improving your website's online presence and search engine performance.

C. Online Reputation Management in Off-Page SEO

Online reputation management (ORM) is a critical component of off-page SEO that involves actively monitoring, influencing, and managing your brand's online image and reputation. In this chapter, we'll delve deep into the realm of online reputation management, exploring its significance, best practices, and strategies to maintain a positive online presence.

1. The Significance of Online Reputation Management

In today's digital age, your brand's reputation is more accessible—and more vulnerable—than ever before. Online reputation management is crucial for several reasons:

- **Trust and Credibility**: A positive online reputation builds trust with your audience, influencing their purchasing decisions and loyalty.

- **Search Engine Rankings**: Online reviews and mentions can impact your website's search engine rankings. Positive mentions can improve rankings, while negative ones can harm them.

- **Customer Relationships**: ORM helps you build and maintain strong customer relationships by addressing concerns and feedback promptly.

- **Competitive Advantage**: Managing your online reputation can set you apart from competitors and strengthen your market position.

2. ORM Strategies and Best Practices

Effective online reputation management involves proactive strategies and best practices:

a. Monitor Mentions

- **Set Up Alerts**: Use tools like Google Alerts, Mention, or social media monitoring tools to receive notifications when your brand is mentioned online.

- **Track Reviews**: Monitor review websites, social media platforms, and industry-specific forums for customer reviews and feedback.

b. Respond Promptly

- **Acknowledge Feedback**: Respond to both positive and negative feedback promptly and professionally. Show appreciation for positive comments, and address concerns in a constructive manner.

- **Apologize and Resolve**: When a customer has a negative experience, acknowledge their concerns, apologize if necessary, and offer solutions to rectify the situation.

c. Encourage Positive Reviews

- **Ask for Reviews**: Encourage satisfied customers to leave reviews on platforms like Google My Business, Yelp, and industry-specific review sites.

- **Provide a Platform**: Make it easy for customers to leave reviews by including links and review instructions on your website and in email communications.

d. Create High-Quality Content

- **Content Strategy**: Publish valuable, informative, and engaging content on your website and social media channels to establish authority and expertise in your industry.

- **Blogging**: Maintain an active blog with content that addresses common questions and pain points in your niche.

e. Social Media Engagement

- **Active Presence**: Maintain an active presence on social media platforms to engage with your audience and address their inquiries and concerns.

- **Positive Messaging**: Share positive stories, testimonials, and updates to reinforce a positive brand image.

f. Address Negative Content

- **Removal or Correction**: If inaccurate or harmful information is published online, work to have it removed or corrected through legal means if necessary.

- **Suppress Negative Results**: Optimize your website and positive content to outrank negative search results in search engine rankings.

g. Online Review and Feedback Platforms

- **Google My Business**: Monitor and respond to reviews on your Google My Business listing, as they can significantly impact local SEO.

- **Yelp**: Maintain an active presence on Yelp and respond to reviews, as Yelp reviews can influence local purchasing decisions.

3. Building a Crisis Management Plan

Prepare for potential online reputation crises by creating a crisis management plan:

- **Identify Potential Issues**: Anticipate potential reputation threats and challenges that could arise in your industry.

- **Designate Responsibility**: Assign roles and responsibilities within your organization for handling reputation crises.

- **Develop a Response Plan**: Establish a clear plan of action for responding to various types of crises, including communication strategies and timelines.

- **Monitor and Assess**: Continuously monitor online mentions and sentiment to identify and address potential issues before they escalate.

4. Leveraging Positive Reviews and Testimonials

Positive reviews and testimonials are valuable assets in ORM:

- **Display on Your Website**: Showcase positive reviews and testimonials prominently on your website to build trust with visitors.

- **Share on Social Media**: Share positive feedback on your social media channels to reinforce a positive brand image.

5. Seek Professional Assistance

If managing your online reputation becomes overwhelming or if you face a severe reputation crisis, consider enlisting the services of an online reputation management agency or specialist with expertise in managing online reputations effectively.

In conclusion, online reputation management is an essential component of off-page SEO that directly influences your brand's trustworthiness, search engine rankings, and customer relationships. By actively monitoring and managing your online reputation, responding to feedback, encouraging positive reviews, and preparing for potential crises, you can build and maintain a strong and positive online presence. As you delve into the strategies and best practices in this chapter, you'll gain the knowledge and skills necessary to master the art of online reputation management and safeguard your brand's reputation in the digital world.

D. Guest Blogging and Influencer Outreach in Off-Page SEO

Guest blogging and influencer outreach are dynamic strategies in the realm of off-page SEO, both aimed at expanding your online presence, building quality backlinks, and increasing your brand's authority. In this chapter, we'll dive deep into these two powerful techniques, exploring their significance, best practices, and how to leverage them effectively for SEO success.

1. Guest Blogging: The Art of Collaboration

Guest blogging, also known as guest posting, is a strategy where you write and publish content on someone else's blog or website. In return, you gain exposure to their audience and often receive a backlink to your website. Here's why guest blogging is significant:

- **Backlinks**: High-quality guest posts can provide valuable backlinks to your website, contributing to your off-page SEO efforts.

- **Audience Expansion**: By writing for a different audience, you can tap into new demographics and potentially gain loyal followers.

- **Authority Building**: Guest blogging on authoritative websites can boost your reputation and authority within your niche.

2. Guest Blogging Best Practices

To succeed in guest blogging, follow these best practices:

a. Target Reputable Websites

- **Relevance**: Choose websites that are relevant to your niche or industry to ensure your content resonates with the audience.

- **Authority**: Prioritize authoritative websites with a strong online presence and a history of quality content.

b. Research and Personalize Pitches

- **Thorough Research**: Familiarize yourself with the target website's content, audience, and style before pitching your ideas.

- **Personalized Pitches**: Craft personalized and compelling pitches that demonstrate your understanding of the host site's needs and audience.

c. High-Quality Content

- **Valuable Content**: Create content that provides

genuine value to the readers of the host site. Address their pain points and offer actionable insights.

• **Originality**: Ensure your content is original, well-researched, and not a duplicate of existing material.

d. Author Bio and Links

• **Detailed Author Bio**: Include a comprehensive author bio that introduces you and your expertise. This is your opportunity to establish credibility.

• **Relevant Links**: Include relevant links to your website or content within the body of the guest post when appropriate.

e. Promote Your Guest Posts

• **Social Sharing**: Share your guest posts on your social media channels to expand their reach.

• **Engage with Comments**: Engage with readers in the comments section of your guest posts to build relationships.

3. Influencer Outreach: Leveraging Authority

Influencer outreach involves connecting with influencers in your niche or industry and collaborating with them to expand your brand's reach and authority. Here's why influencer outreach is significant:

- **Audience Reach**: Influencers have dedicated and engaged followers who trust their recommendations.

- **Credibility**: Partnering with influencers lends credibility and authority to your brand.

- **Content Amplification**: Influencers can help amplify your content and messages to a wider audience.

4. Influencer Outreach Best Practices

To make the most of influencer outreach, follow these best practices:

a. Identify Relevant Influencers

- **Niche Alignment**: Choose influencers whose niche and audience align with your brand.

- **Audience Engagement**: Assess the level of engagement and authenticity of an influencer's audience.

b. Build Genuine Relationships

- **Personalized Outreach**: Craft personalized and sincere outreach messages. Avoid generic or spammy pitches.

- **Mutual Benefit**: Highlight the mutual benefits of collaboration and how it can add value to the influencer's audience.

c. Collaborate Authentically

- **Authentic Content**: Collaborate with influencers on authentic and valuable content that resonates with their audience.

- **Transparency**: Be transparent about the nature of the collaboration and any compensation involved.

d. Leverage Various Platforms

- **Social Media**: Collaborate with influencers on social media campaigns, giveaways, or sponsored posts.

- **Content Co-Creation**: Collaborate on blog posts, videos, webinars, or podcasts to reach a broader audience.

e. Measure and Analyze

- **Performance Metrics**: Use analytics to measure the performance of influencer collaborations. Assess reach, engagement, and conversions.

- **Feedback**: Seek feedback from influencers on how to improve future collaborations.

5. Influencer Outreach Tools

There are several tools and platforms that can help streamline influencer outreach and management, such as BuzzSumo, Traackr, and AspireIQ. These tools can assist in identifying potential influencers, managing relationships, and tracking campaign performance.

In conclusion, guest blogging and influencer outreach are potent off-page SEO strategies that can enhance your online presence, build quality backlinks, and establish your brand's authority. By adhering to best practices, conducting thorough research, and fostering genuine relationships, you can effectively leverage these techniques to achieve SEO success and expand your brand's reach. As you explore these strategies in this chapter, you'll gain the knowledge and skills necessary to harness the power of guest blogging and influencer outreach in the competitive digital landscape.

E. The Role of Content Marketing in Off-Page SEO

Content marketing is a cornerstone of off-page SEO that revolves around creating and distributing high-quality, relevant content to engage and attract a target audience. In this chapter, we'll explore the pivotal role of content marketing in off-page SEO, understanding its significance, best practices, and how it can enhance your website's visibility, authority, and overall search engine optimization efforts.

1. The Significance of Content Marketing in Off-Page SEO

Content marketing plays a vital role in off-page SEO for several compelling reasons:

- **Quality Backlinks**: High-quality content attracts natural backlinks from authoritative websites, improving your backlink profile.

- **User Engagement**: Engaging and informative content fosters user engagement, encouraging visitors to spend more time on your website.

- **Brand Authority**: Consistently publishing valuable content positions your brand as an authoritative source in your niche or industry.

- **Social Signals**: Shareable content generates social media signals, contributing to your website's online presence and authority.

- **Increased Visibility**: High-quality content ranks well in search engines, increasing your website's visibility and attracting organic traffic.

2. Content Marketing Best Practices

To harness the power of content marketing for off-page SEO, follow these best practices:

a. Audience-Centric Approach

- **Know Your Audience**: Understand your target audience's needs, pain points, and interests to create content that resonates with them.

- **Buyer Personas**: Develop detailed buyer personas to guide your content creation efforts.

b. High-Quality, Valuable Content

- **Originality**: Create original and unique content that offers fresh insights or perspectives.

- **Relevance**: Ensure your content addresses relevant topics and provides solutions to common queries within your niche.

- **Depth**: Dive deep into topics, providing comprehensive coverage and in-depth analysis when necessary.

c. Content Variety

- **Blog Posts**: Maintain an active blog with regular posts addressing various aspects of your niche.

- **Visual Content**: Incorporate visuals like infographics, videos, and images to make your content more engaging.

- **Ebooks and Whitepapers**: Offer downloadable

resources that provide valuable information in exchange for visitor information.

d. SEO Optimization

- **Keyword Research**: Conduct keyword research to identify relevant keywords and phrases to target in your content.

- **On-Page SEO**: Optimize your content for on-page SEO elements like title tags, meta descriptions, headers, and internal links.

- **Structured Data**: Implement structured data (schema markup) to enhance search engine visibility and click-through rates.

e. Content Promotion

- **Social Media**: Share your content on social media platforms to reach a broader audience and encourage social signals.

- **Email Marketing**: Promote your content through email newsletters to engage with your existing audience.

- **Guest Blogging**: Collaborate with reputable websites to publish guest posts that link back to your valuable content.

f. Metrics and Analytics

- **Track Performance**: Use analytics tools like Google Analytics to measure the performance of your content, including traffic, engagement, and conversions.

- **Iterate and Improve**: Continuously analyze performance data and use insights to refine your content marketing strategy.

3. Evergreen and Timely Content

- **Evergreen Content**: Create evergreen content that remains relevant over time. Evergreen articles continue to attract traffic and backlinks long after publication.

- **Timely Content**: Stay current by addressing timely topics and trends within your niche. Timely content can generate immediate traffic and engagement.

4. Content Calendar and Consistency

- **Content Calendar**: Develop a content calendar to plan and organize your content creation efforts. Consistency in publishing is key.

- **Quality Over Quantity**: Prioritize quality over quantity. It's better to produce fewer pieces of high-quality content than to publish low-value content frequently.

5. User Experience

- **Mobile-Friendly**: Ensure your content is mobile-friendly, as an increasing number of users access content via mobile devices.

- **Fast Loading**: Optimize page load times to improve user experience and reduce bounce rates.

6. Building Relationships

- **Collaboration**: Collaborate with influencers, industry experts, and other content creators in your niche to expand your reach and build relationships.

- **Community Engagement**: Engage with your audience through comments, forums, and social media to foster a sense of community and loyalty.

In conclusion, content marketing is a fundamental element of off-page SEO that can significantly enhance your website's visibility, authority, and user engagement. By adhering to best practices, producing high-quality, audience-centric content, and continuously analyzing performance data, you can create a content marketing strategy that strengthens your online presence and drives organic traffic. As you delve into these strategies in this chapter, you'll gain the knowledge and skills necessary to harness the power of content marketing in the competitive digital

Mastering Search Engine Optimization (SEO)

landscape.

Chapter 6:

Technical SEO

Technical SEO forms the backbone of your website's search engine optimization strategy. In this chapter, we embark on a journey into the intricate world of technical SEO, where we explore the critical aspects, best practices, and advanced techniques that enable search engines to crawl, index, and rank your website effectively. From website speed optimization to structured data implementation, you'll gain a deep understanding of the technical underpinnings that can propel your website to the top of search engine results.

A. Website Speed and Page Load Times

Website speed and page load times are pivotal components of technical SEO. In this section, we delve deep into the importance of website speed, its impact on user experience and search engine rankings, and the strategies and techniques to optimize your website's performance for faster load times.

1. The Significance of Website Speed in Technical SEO

Website speed is not just a user experience concern; it's a

critical ranking factor in search engine algorithms. Here's why website speed is of paramount importance:

- **User Experience**: Faster-loading websites provide a superior user experience, reducing bounce rates and improving engagement.

- **Search Engine Rankings**: Google and other search engines consider page load times when ranking websites. Faster websites are more likely to rank higher in search results.

- **Mobile Friendliness**: With the proliferation of mobile devices, fast load times are even more critical for mobile users.

- **Conversion Rates**: Speed impacts conversion rates directly. Slower websites tend to have lower conversion rates, affecting your bottom line.

2. Measuring Website Speed

Before you can optimize your website's speed, you need to measure it. Several tools and metrics help gauge your website's performance:

- **PageSpeed Insights**: Google's PageSpeed Insights tool provides a comprehensive analysis of your website's speed and offers suggestions for improvement.

- **GTmetrix**: GTmetrix analyzes your website's speed

performance, provides scores, and identifies areas for optimization.

- **Pingdom**: Pingdom offers a website speed test that allows you to check the load time of your web pages from various locations worldwide.

3. Strategies to Improve Website Speed

To enhance your website's speed and page load times, consider the following strategies:

a. Image Optimization

- **Compress Images**: Use image compression tools to reduce the file size of images without sacrificing quality.

- **Image Formats**: Choose appropriate image formats (JPEG, PNG, WebP) for different types of images.

- **Lazy Loading**: Implement lazy loading to load images as users scroll down the page, reducing initial load times.

b. Minimize HTTP Requests

- **Combine Files**: Minimize the number of HTTP requests by combining CSS and JavaScript files.

- **Use CSS Sprites**: Combine multiple images into a single image sprite to reduce image requests.

c. Content Delivery Network (CDN)

- **CDN Integration**: Utilize a CDN to distribute your website's content to servers located closer to users, reducing latency.

d. Browser Caching

- **Leverage Browser Caching**: Set up browser caching to store static resources on the user's device, reducing load times for returning visitors.

e. Minify Code

- **Code Compression**: Minify HTML, CSS, and JavaScript to remove unnecessary spaces, line breaks, and comments, reducing file sizes.

f. Server Optimization

- **Quality Hosting**: Choose a reliable and fast web hosting provider to ensure your server responds quickly.

- **HTTP/2 Protocol**: Use the HTTP/2 protocol to enable faster data transfer between the server and the user's browser.

g. Content Delivery Optimization

- **Content Prioritization**: Prioritize the loading of critical content (above-the-fold) to enhance perceived speed.

- **Asynchronous Loading**: Load non-essential content asynchronously to prevent it from blocking the rendering of the page.

h. Mobile Optimization

- **Responsive Design**: Implement responsive design to ensure your website loads quickly and effectively on mobile devices.

- **Accelerated Mobile Pages (AMP)**: Consider using AMP for mobile pages to deliver ultra-fast mobile experiences.

i. Monitoring and Testing

- **Regular Testing**: Continuously monitor and test your website's speed using the aforementioned tools and metrics.

- **A/B Testing**: Conduct A/B testing to assess the impact of speed improvements on user engagement and conversion rates.

4. Measuring the Impact

To understand the impact of your speed optimization efforts, track key performance indicators (KPIs) such as:

- **Page Load Time**: Measure the time it takes for your web pages to load.

- **Bounce Rate**: Monitor the percentage of users who

leave your site without engaging due to slow load times.

- **Conversion Rates**: Observe changes in conversion rates as a result of speed improvements.

- **Search Engine Rankings**: Monitor your website's search engine rankings as speed optimizations may positively impact your positions in search results.

5. Ongoing Maintenance

Website speed is not a one-time task; it requires ongoing maintenance. Regularly revisit and test your website's speed to ensure it continues to provide a fast and efficient user experience.

In conclusion, website speed and page load times are integral to technical SEO and user experience. By implementing the strategies and techniques outlined in this section, you can optimize your website's performance, improve search engine rankings, enhance user engagement, and ultimately, drive better results for your online presence. As you explore these strategies in this chapter, you'll gain the knowledge and skills necessary to master the art of website speed optimization.

B. XML Sitemaps and Robots.txt

XML sitemaps and robots.txt files are essential elements of technical SEO that facilitate search engine crawling, indexing, and the overall optimization of your website's visibility in search results. In this section, we will delve deep into the significance of XML sitemaps and robots.txt files, understanding their roles, best practices, and how they contribute to the health and performance of your website in search engines.

1. XML Sitemaps: A Roadmap for Crawlers

XML sitemaps are digital maps of your website's content structure, designed explicitly for search engines. Here's why XML sitemaps are crucial in technical SEO:

• **Crawler Guidance**: XML sitemaps provide search engine crawlers with a clear roadmap of your website's structure, helping them discover and index content efficiently.

• **Indexation Control**: You can specify which pages to include or exclude from the sitemap, giving you control over what gets indexed.

• **Fresh Content Notification**: XML sitemaps can notify search engines of newly published content, ensuring timely indexing.

• **Error Identification**: Sitemaps can highlight crawl errors, such as broken links or inaccessible pages, allowing you to address them promptly.

2. Creating an XML Sitemap

To create an XML sitemap, follow these steps:

a. Use Sitemap Generators: Numerous online tools and plugins are available to generate XML sitemaps automatically. Popular platforms like WordPress often have plugins that simplify this process.

b. Manually Generate: For more control, you can manually create an XML sitemap using XML syntax. However, this method is best suited for advanced users.

c. Include Essential Pages: Ensure your XML sitemap includes essential pages like your homepage, key landing pages, blog posts, and product/service pages.

d. Regular Updates: Keep your XML sitemap up to date by adding new pages and removing deprecated ones.

e. Submit to Search Engines: Once your XML sitemap is generated, submit it to search engines through their respective webmaster tools, such as Google Search Console and Bing Webmaster Tools.

3. Robots.txt: Managing Crawler Access

Robots.txt is a text file that instructs search engine crawlers on which parts of your website should be crawled and indexed and which should be excluded. Here's why robots.txt files are significant in technical SEO:

- **Crawler Efficiency**: Robots.txt helps crawlers prioritize crawling the most important and relevant pages of your site.

- **Privacy Control**: It can prevent sensitive or private information from appearing in search results.

- **Resource Savings**: By excluding non-essential pages or directories from crawling, you can save server resources.

4. Creating a Robots.txt File

To create a robots.txt file, follow these best practices:

a. Proper Placement: Place the robots.txt file in the root directory of your website (e.g., **www.yourwebsite.com/robots.txt**).

b. Clear Directives: Use clear directives to specify which user-agents (crawlers) are allowed or disallowed from accessing specific parts of your website.

c. User-Agent Specifications: Include user-agent specifications for major search engines like Googlebot and Bingbot.

d. Directory Exclusions: You can exclude entire directories (e.g., /images/) or individual pages (e.g., /private-page/) from crawling.

e. Wildcards: Utilize wildcards (*) *to apply rules to a group of pages. For instance, "Disallow: /blog/"* would disallow crawling of all pages under the /blog/ directory.

5. Regular Review and Testing

• Regularly review and test your robots.txt file to ensure it's working as intended. Use tools like Google's Robots Testing Tool to check for any issues.

6. Sitemap and Robots.txt Relationship

XML sitemaps and robots.txt files can work together harmoniously:

• You can reference your XML sitemap in your robots.txt file to inform crawlers of its existence. For example: "Sitemap: **https://www.yourwebsite.com/sitemap.xml**".

• Ensure that there are no conflicting directives in your robots.txt that would disallow access to URLs included in your XML sitemap.

In conclusion, XML sitemaps and robots.txt files are indispensable tools in technical SEO that facilitate efficient crawling, indexing, and control over your website's visibility in search engines. By understanding their roles, following best practices, and regularly reviewing and updating these files, you can optimize your website's performance and ensure that search engines can navigate your site effectively. As you explore these strategies in this chapter, you'll gain the knowledge and skills necessary to master the management of XML sitemaps and robots.txt files for the benefit of your website's search engine optimization.

C. Canonicalization and Duplicate Content

Canonicalization and addressing duplicate content are fundamental aspects of technical SEO. In this section, we will explore the significance of canonicalization, the challenges posed by duplicate content, best practices, and how to ensure that search engines index the right versions of your web pages.

1. Canonicalization: Directing Search Engines to the Preferred Page

Canonicalization is a technique used to guide search engines to the preferred version of a web page when multiple versions of similar or identical content exist. Here's why canonicalization is essential:

- **Duplicate Content Avoidance**: It prevents issues associated with duplicate content, such as ranking dilution and potential penalties from search engines.

- **Consolidation of Signals**: Canonicalization consolidates ranking signals like backlinks, social shares, and engagement metrics to the preferred page.

- **Optimized User Experience**: It enhances the user experience by ensuring that visitors land on the most relevant page.

2. Types of Duplicate Content

Duplicate content can manifest in various forms, including:

a. Exact Duplicate Content: Identical content found on multiple URLs.

b. Near-Duplicate Content: Content that is nearly identical but includes minor variations.

c. Printer-Friendly and Mobile Versions: Separate URLs for print or mobile versions of pages that contain substantially the same content.

d. URL Parameters: Different URLs with the same content due to URL parameters.

3. Implementing Canonical Tags

To address duplicate content issues, canonical tags

(rel="canonical") are added to the HTML head of web pages. Here's how to implement them:

a. Identify the Preferred Page: Determine which version of the content you want search engines to consider as the canonical version.

b. Insert the Canonical Tag: Add the canonical tag to the HTML head section of the non-canonical pages, specifying the preferred (canonical) URL. For example:

```
<link rel="canonical"
href="https://www.yourwebsite.com/preferred-page" />
```

c. Use Absolute URLs: Always use absolute URLs in the canonical tag to avoid ambiguity.

d. Consistency: Ensure that the canonical tag is consistent across all versions of the page, including HTTP/HTTPS, www/non-www, and language versions.

4. Handling Complex Canonicalization Scenarios

Canonicalization can become more complex in scenarios like pagination or parameter-driven content. Here are strategies for addressing these cases:

a. Pagination: For paginated content, use rel="prev" and rel="next" tags to indicate the sequence of pages, and specify the canonical version on the first page.

b. Parameter Handling: Utilize URL parameters carefully. Use Google's URL Parameters tool in Google Search Console to instruct search engines on parameter handling.

5. The Role of 301 Redirects

In some cases, 301 redirects are used instead of canonical tags to address duplicate content issues. Redirects permanently direct users and search engines from one URL to another, effectively consolidating the content.

6. Duplicate Content and International SEO

Addressing duplicate content is particularly important in international SEO. Implement hreflang tags to indicate language and regional targeting, and ensure that canonical tags are used consistently across language and regional versions of your site.

7. Monitoring and Maintenance

Regularly monitor your website for potential duplicate content issues using tools like Google Search Console. Periodically review and update canonical tags as needed, especially when making changes to your website's structure or content.

8. SEO Tools and Resources

Several SEO tools and resources can assist in identifying and addressing duplicate content issues, including Copyscape, Screaming Frog SEO Spider, and Google Search Console.

In summary, canonicalization and addressing duplicate content are critical for maintaining a healthy and effective technical SEO strategy. By implementing canonical tags, handling complex scenarios, and monitoring your website's performance, you can ensure that search engines index the right versions of your web pages and prevent issues associated with duplicate content. As you explore these strategies in this chapter, you'll gain the knowledge and skills necessary to master canonicalization and effectively manage duplicate content for the benefit of your website's search engine optimization.

D. Schema Markup and Rich Snippets

Schema markup, often referred to as structured data, and rich snippets are powerful tools in the arsenal of technical SEO. In this section, we'll explore the significance of schema markup, how it enhances your website's visibility in search results, best practices, and the impact of rich snippets on user engagement.

1. Schema Markup: Enhancing Content for Search Engines

Schema markup is a form of structured data that you can add to your website's HTML to provide search engines with additional context about your content. Here's why schema markup is essential in technical SEO:

- **Improved Search Results**: Schema markup helps search engines understand the content of your pages better, leading to more informative and visually appealing search results.

- **Rich Snippets**: It enables the creation of rich snippets that provide users with enhanced information directly in the search results, improving click-through rates.

- **Semantic SEO**: Schema markup enhances semantic SEO by connecting content elements to their semantic meaning, making it easier for search engines to interpret and index.

2. Types of Schema Markup

There are various types of schema markup available to mark up different types of content, including:

a. Product: Used for e-commerce product listings, including product names, prices, and availability.

b. Article: Provides details about news articles, blog posts, and other textual content, including headline, date published, and author.

c. Local Business: Marks up information about local businesses, including address, phone number, and operating hours.

d. Review: Used to showcase user reviews and ratings for products, services, or businesses.

e. Event: Provides details about events, including date, time, location, and ticket information.

f. FAQ: Marks up frequently asked questions and answers on your website.

g. Video: Used for video content, providing information like duration, thumbnail, and video description.

3. Implementing Schema Markup

To implement schema markup effectively, follow these best practices:

a. Choose Relevant Markup: Select the appropriate schema markup type that aligns with the content on your web page.

b. Markup the Entire Page: Apply schema markup to the entire page, covering all relevant content elements.

c. Use Schema Markup Generators: Utilize schema markup generators or testing tools provided by search engines to create and validate your schema markup.

d. Add Markup to HTML: Insert the schema markup code into the HTML of your page, typically in the head or body section.

e. Test Your Markup: After implementation, use Google's Structured Data Testing Tool to ensure your schema markup is correctly formatted and recognized.

f. Monitor Changes: Keep an eye on changes and updates to schema markup standards to stay up-to-date with best practices.

4. Rich Snippets: Enhanced Search Results

Rich snippets are the visual enhancements that appear in search results, providing additional information beyond the standard title and meta description. These can include star ratings, product prices, event dates, and more. Rich snippets serve the following purposes:

- **Improved Click-Through Rates**: Rich snippets make search results more attractive and informative, increasing the likelihood of users clicking on your link.

- **Enhanced User Experience**: Users can quickly gather essential information from the search results page without visiting the actual webpage.

5. Common Types of Rich Snippets

Common types of rich snippets include:

a. Review Stars: Displays user ratings and reviews for products, services, or businesses.

b. Product Information: Provides product details such as price, availability, and product ratings.

c. Events: Shows event details such as dates, times, and locations.

d. Recipe Cards: Displays cooking times, ingredients, and calorie counts for recipes.

e. Q&A Snippets: Features frequently asked questions and their corresponding answers.

f. Breadcrumbs: Shows the site's page hierarchy in search results.

g. Video Thumbnails: Displays video thumbnails alongside video search results.

6. Impact of Rich Snippets on User Engagement

Rich snippets have a significant impact on user engagement:

- **Increased Click-Through Rates**: Studies have shown that rich snippets can lead to higher click-through rates as users are more likely to click on visually appealing and informative search results.

- **Improved User Experience**: Users appreciate the convenience of getting relevant information directly from the search results page, saving them time and effort.

- **Better Informed Choices**: Rich snippets help users make more informed decisions, such as choosing the right product or deciding whether to attend an event.

7. Implementing Rich Snippets

To enable rich snippets for your web pages, follow these steps:

a. Implement Schema Markup: As previously discussed, schema markup is the foundation for rich snippets. Ensure that you've correctly applied schema markup to your content.

b. Validate Your Markup: Use Google's Structured Data Testing Tool to validate your schema markup and check for any errors or warnings.

c. Submit to Google: If you're using specific types of rich snippets like recipe cards or event information, you can submit these to Google through Google Search Console to expedite indexing.

d. Monitor Performance: After implementing rich snippets, monitor your search engine performance, and assess the impact on click-through rates and user engagement.

In conclusion, schema markup and rich snippets are indispensable tools in technical SEO that enhance the visibility of your content in search results and improve user engagement. By effectively implementing schema markup, choosing the right types of rich snippets, and monitoring their impact, you can optimize your website's search engine performance and provide users with informative and engaging search results. As you explore these strategies in this chapter, you'll gain the knowledge and skills necessary to harness the power of schema markup and rich snippets for the benefit of your website's search engine optimization.

E. HTTPS and Security Considerations

HTTPS (Hypertext Transfer Protocol Secure) and security considerations are paramount in today's digital landscape. In this section, we'll explore the significance of HTTPS, its impact on SEO and user trust, best practices for implementation, and broader security considerations for safeguarding your website and user data.

1. HTTPS: The Secure Web Connection

HTTPS is an extension of the standard HTTP protocol but with added security features. It encrypts the data exchanged between a user's web browser and a website's server, protecting it from eavesdropping, data tampering, and other security threats.

2. The Significance of HTTPS in SEO

HTTPS has a direct impact on SEO and user trust. Here's why

it's crucial:

- **Search Engine Ranking**: Google considers HTTPS as a ranking signal, meaning that websites using HTTPS tend to rank higher in search results.

- **User Trust**: Users are more likely to trust websites that display the padlock symbol (indicating a secure connection) in the address bar.

- **Data Protection**: HTTPS encrypts data transmitted between the user and the website, safeguarding sensitive information such as login credentials and payment details.

3. Implementing HTTPS: Best Practices

To implement HTTPS effectively, follow these best practices:

a. Secure SSL/TLS Certificate: Acquire a trusted SSL/TLS certificate from a reputable Certificate Authority (CA). Choose the right certificate type (e.g., DV, OV, EV) based on your website's needs.

b. Installation: Install the SSL/TLS certificate on your web server following the CA's instructions or using the hosting provider's tools.

c. Configure HTTPS: Ensure your website is properly configured to use HTTPS. Update internal links, resources, and references to use the "https://" protocol.

d. Redirect HTTP to HTTPS: Implement a 301 redirect to automatically redirect HTTP requests to HTTPS. This prevents duplicate content issues and ensures a seamless user experience.

e. Mixed Content: Avoid mixed content issues by ensuring all resources (images, scripts, stylesheets) on your website are loaded via HTTPS. Mixed content can trigger browser warnings and compromise security.

f. HSTS (HTTP Strict Transport Security): Implement HSTS to instruct browsers to only access your website over HTTPS, even if users enter "http://" in the address bar.

g. Content Security Policy (CSP): Implement a CSP to mitigate cross-site scripting (XSS) attacks by specifying trusted sources for content and scripts.

h. Test and Monitor: Regularly test your HTTPS setup and monitor it for security vulnerabilities and potential issues.

4. Broader Security Considerations

Beyond HTTPS, consider these broader security considerations to protect your website and user data:

a. Web Application Firewall (WAF): Implement a WAF to filter and block malicious traffic and attacks, such as SQL injection and DDoS attacks.

b. Regular Backups: Perform regular backups of your website's data and code. Store backups securely, and test their restoration process.

c. Strong Password Policies: Enforce strong password policies for user accounts and regularly update administrative passwords.

d. Security Updates: Keep your web server, CMS (e.g., WordPress, Drupal), plugins, and themes up to date with the latest security patches.

e. Security Headers: Add security headers (e.g., X-Content-Type-Options, X-Frame-Options, Content Security Policy) to your website's HTTP responses to enhance security.

f. User Data Protection: If your website collects user data, ensure compliance with data protection regulations (e.g., GDPR) and employ robust data encryption and protection measures.

g. User Education: Educate your team and users about security best practices, including recognizing phishing attempts and maintaining strong passwords.

h. Incident Response Plan: Develop an incident response plan to address security breaches swiftly and effectively.

i. Regular Audits and Penetration Testing: Conduct regular security audits and penetration testing to identify vulnerabilities and weaknesses.

j. Third-Party Integrations: Review the security practices of third-party services and integrations used on your website.

k. Secure File Uploads: If your website allows file uploads, implement security measures to prevent malicious uploads.

5. Continuous Monitoring and Response

Security is an ongoing process. Continuously monitor your website's security, stay informed about emerging threats, and adapt your security measures accordingly. Develop a response plan to address security incidents promptly and effectively.

In conclusion, HTTPS and security considerations are integral to technical SEO and the overall safety of your website and user data. By implementing HTTPS using best practices, addressing broader security concerns, and maintaining a vigilant security posture, you can enhance your website's visibility, user trust, and protection against potential threats. As you explore these strategies in this chapter, you'll gain the knowledge and skills necessary to master HTTPS and security considerations for the benefit of your website's search engine optimization and overall security.

Chapter 7:

Local SEO

Local SEO is a specialized facet of search engine optimization that focuses on optimizing a business's online presence to improve its visibility in local search results. In this chapter, we'll explore the fundamental concepts of local SEO, its significance for brick-and-mortar and service-based businesses, and the strategies that can help businesses thrive in their local markets. Whether you're a local business owner or an SEO professional, this chapter will equip you with the knowledge and techniques needed to excel in local SEO and attract nearby customers.

A. The Importance of Local Search

Local search has evolved into a critical component of online visibility and marketing for businesses, especially those with physical locations or a local customer base. In this section, we'll delve into the profound importance of local search, its impact on businesses, and why prioritizing local SEO strategies is essential in the digital age.

1. The Shift to Local Search

The internet has profoundly changed the way consumers find and engage with businesses. Local search refers to the practice of searching for products, services, or information with a specific geographic intent. Consider the following factors that highlight the shift towards local search:

- **Mobile Devices**: The prevalence of smartphones means that people can search for businesses and services on-the-go, often with location-based services enabled.

- **Voice Search**: The rise of voice-activated digital assistants like Siri and Google Assistant has made local search even more prevalent.

- **Consumer Behavior**: Consumers increasingly use search engines to discover local businesses, read reviews, compare prices, and get directions.

- **Google's Focus**: Search engines like Google have adapted to this shift, prioritizing local search results through features like Google Maps and the "local pack."

2. The Impact of Local Search on Businesses

The significance of local search for businesses cannot be overstated:

- **Visibility**: Local search helps businesses become more visible to potential customers in their immediate vicinity, which can significantly impact foot traffic and revenue.

- **Trust and Credibility**: Having a strong online presence in local search results builds trust and credibility with consumers who rely on reviews and ratings.

- **Competitive Edge**: Optimizing for local search provides a competitive advantage, especially for smaller businesses competing against larger corporations.

- **Consumer Behavior**: Studies show that consumers increasingly rely on online information to make informed purchasing decisions, including choices about where to shop and dine locally.

- **Multi-Channel Impact**: Local SEO not only affects search engine results but also impacts other channels like social media, online directories, and mobile apps.

3. Targeting Local vs. National/Global Audiences

Local SEO is distinct from national or global SEO in that it focuses on a specific geographic area. Businesses that cater to local audiences must recognize this distinction and prioritize local SEO for several reasons:

- **Relevance**: Local search ensures that businesses are

relevant to their immediate communities, aligning with the intent of local consumers.

- **Cost-Efficiency**: Local SEO can be more cost-effective than broader, national campaigns, particularly for small businesses.

- **Engagement**: Localized content and promotions are more engaging and relatable to local audiences.

- **Consumer Behavior**: Many consumers prefer local businesses for convenience, trust, and the sense of supporting their community.

4. The Role of Google My Business

Google My Business (GMB) is a pivotal element of local SEO. It's a free tool provided by Google that enables businesses to manage their online presence on Google Search and Google Maps. GMB offers several benefits:

- **Listing Information**: Businesses can provide essential information like their name, address, phone number, hours of operation, and website URL.

- **Reviews and Ratings**: Customers can leave reviews and ratings, which can influence potential customers' decisions.

- **Photos and Posts**: Businesses can upload photos and

post updates to engage with their audience.

- **Local Pack**: GMB listings often appear in the "local pack," a prominent display of local businesses on the search results page.

5. The Importance of NAP Consistency

NAP stands for Name, Address, and Phone number. NAP consistency refers to ensuring that this information is uniform across all online platforms, including your website, GMB listing, online directories, and social media profiles. Inconsistent NAP information can confuse search engines and potential customers, negatively impacting your local search rankings and reputation.

In conclusion, the importance of local search cannot be underestimated in today's digital landscape. Local SEO is not just a strategy; it's a necessity for businesses aiming to thrive in their local markets. By recognizing the shift towards local search, understanding its impact on businesses, and effectively optimizing for local SEO, businesses can enjoy increased visibility, trust, and engagement with their local customer base. As you explore the strategies in this chapter, you'll gain the knowledge and skills necessary to master local SEO and propel your business to success in your local community.

B. Google My Business Optimization

Google My Business (GMB) is a powerful tool for local businesses seeking to enhance their online presence and connect with local customers. In this section, we'll explore the importance of optimizing your Google My Business listing, the steps to do so effectively, and the impact it can have on your local SEO and customer engagement.

1. The Significance of Google My Business

Google My Business is a free and essential platform for local businesses that offers numerous benefits:

- **Online Visibility**: A well-optimized GMB listing helps your business appear prominently in local search results, including the local pack and Google Maps.

- **Information Hub**: It serves as a centralized hub for crucial business information, such as your business name, address, phone number, website, and hours of operation.

- **Customer Engagement**: GMB enables direct engagement with your customers through reviews, posts, and messages, fostering trust and loyalty.

- **Insights and Analytics**: GMB provides valuable insights into how customers find your business, what they do once they land on your listing, and more.

2. Steps for Google My Business Optimization

To optimize your GMB listing effectively, follow these steps:

a. Claim and Verify Your Listing: If you haven't already, claim your GMB listing and verify it with Google. Verification options include mail, phone, email, and instant verification for eligible businesses.

b. Complete Your Profile: Provide comprehensive and accurate information, including your business name, address, phone number (NAP), website URL, categories, and hours of operation. Ensure that your NAP is consistent with your website and other online platforms.

c. Write an Engaging Business Description: Craft a concise and engaging business description that highlights your unique selling points, services, and what sets your business apart.

d. Add High-Quality Photos: Upload high-resolution images of your business, including the exterior, interior, products, services, team, and any special offerings. Use professional photos to showcase your business in the best light.

e. Gather and Manage Reviews: Encourage satisfied customers to leave reviews on your GMB listing. Respond to reviews promptly, thanking customers for positive feedback and addressing any negative comments professionally.

f. Post Regular Updates: Use the "Posts" feature to share updates, promotions, events, and news about your business. These posts appear directly in your listing and can engage potential customers.

g. Frequently Update Information: Keep your listing current by updating information like holiday hours, special hours, and service offerings. Ensure that your listing reflects any changes in your business.

h. Use Attributes: Take advantage of attributes to provide additional information about your business, such as whether you offer outdoor seating, Wi-Fi, or wheelchair accessibility.

i. Monitor Insights: Regularly review the insights and analytics provided by GMB to understand how customers are finding and interacting with your listing. Use this data to refine your strategies.

3. Leveraging Google My Business for SEO

Optimizing your GMB listing also impacts your local SEO efforts:

- **Local Pack Rankings**: A well-optimized GMB listing can improve your rankings in the local pack, a prominent display of local businesses in search results.

- **Increased Click-Through Rates**: Engaging content,

such as high-quality photos and posts, can lead to higher click-through rates from search results.

- **Relevance and Trust**: Google uses information from GMB listings to assess the relevance and trustworthiness of your business, which can impact your overall search rankings.

- **Voice Search**: Voice-activated assistants often rely on GMB information to provide local business recommendations, so optimizing your listing can enhance your visibility in voice search results.

4. Managing Multiple Locations

For businesses with multiple locations, Google My Business offers a bulk management feature that allows you to manage all your listings from a single dashboard. This simplifies the optimization process and ensures consistency across all locations.

5. Regular Maintenance and Updates

Google My Business optimization is an ongoing process. Regularly update your listing with new photos, posts, and accurate information. Monitor reviews and respond to customer inquiries promptly. Stay informed about new GMB features and incorporate them into your strategy.

In conclusion, optimizing your Google My Business listing is a vital component of local SEO and a powerful way to connect with local customers. By following best practices, providing accurate information, engaging with customers, and using GMB insights to refine your strategy, you can enhance your online visibility and grow your local business. As you explore the strategies in this section, you'll gain the knowledge and skills necessary to master Google My Business optimization and leverage its potential for the benefit of your business's local SEO efforts.

C. Local Citations and NAP Consistency

Local citations and maintaining NAP (Name, Address, Phone number) consistency are integral aspects of local SEO that directly impact a business's online visibility and reputation. In this section, we'll explore the importance of local citations, the role of NAP consistency, strategies for citation management, and how these practices can enhance your local SEO efforts.

1. The Significance of Local Citations

Local citations are online references to your business's NAP information on external websites and directories. These references play a crucial role in local SEO for several reasons:

• **Trust and Credibility**: Consistent and accurate citations build trust with search engines and consumers. Inaccurate or inconsistent citations can lead to confusion and distrust.

- **Local Pack Rankings**: Citations are a significant factor in local pack rankings. A business with a strong citation profile is more likely to appear in the local pack, a prominent display in search results.

- **Wider Online Presence**: Citations expand your online presence beyond your website, making it easier for potential customers to find you in various places across the web.

- **Validation of Business Existence**: Search engines use citations to validate the existence and legitimacy of a business. Multiple consistent citations enhance your business's credibility.

2. The Role of NAP Consistency

NAP consistency refers to the uniformity of your business's Name, Address, and Phone number across all online platforms, including your website, Google My Business, social media profiles, and online directories. Consistency is essential for the following reasons:

- **Search Engine Trust**: Inconsistent NAP information can confuse search engines and affect your local SEO rankings negatively.

- **User Experience**: Consistent NAP ensures that users can find accurate information about your business, including its physical location and contact details.

- **Avoiding Penalties**: Inconsistent NAP information can lead to penalties from search engines, potentially harming your online visibility.

3. Strategies for Citation Management

Effective citation management is essential for local SEO success. Here are strategies to help you manage your citations:

a. Audit Existing Citations: Begin by conducting an audit of your existing citations. Identify any inaccuracies, inconsistencies, or missing citations.

b. Create a Master List: Compile a master list of all your business information, including the official business name, address, phone number, website URL, and other relevant details.

c. Claim and Update Citations: Claim and update your listings on popular online directories and review sites, such as Yelp, Yellow Pages, and TripAdvisor. Ensure that the information is consistent with your master list.

d. Build New Citations: Identify authoritative and industry-specific directories where you can create new citations. Ensure that the NAP information matches your master list.

e. Monitor and Maintain: Continuously monitor your

citations for accuracy. When you make changes to your business's information (e.g., moving to a new location or updating the phone number), update your citations promptly.

f. Tools and Services: Consider using citation management tools and services that can help automate the process of claiming, updating, and monitoring citations.

g. Local Structured Data Markup: Implement local structured data markup (schema markup) on your website to provide search engines with clear NAP information.

4. The Impact of Online Reviews

Online reviews are closely tied to local citations and NAP consistency. Encourage satisfied customers to leave reviews on your Google My Business listing and other relevant review platforms. Positive reviews can enhance your online reputation and local SEO rankings.

5. Handling Multiple Locations

If your business has multiple locations, ensure that you maintain consistent NAP information for each location. Consider using location-specific landing pages on your website to provide relevant information.

6. Local SEO and Mobile Devices

Local citations and NAP consistency are particularly important for mobile users who often use their devices to find local businesses. Optimize your citations and NAP information to cater to mobile searchers.

In conclusion, local citations and NAP consistency are foundational elements of successful local SEO. By actively managing your citations, ensuring NAP consistency across all online platforms, and monitoring your online reviews, you can boost your local search rankings, enhance your online reputation, and make it easier for potential customers to find and contact your business. As you explore these strategies in this section, you'll gain the knowledge and skills necessary to master citation management and NAP consistency for the benefit of your local SEO efforts.

D. Customer Reviews and Ratings

Customer reviews and ratings are pivotal components of local SEO and online reputation management. In this section, we'll explore the significance of customer reviews and ratings, how they impact local search rankings and user trust, strategies for garnering positive reviews, and best practices for managing online reputation effectively.

1. The Significance of Customer Reviews and Ratings

Customer reviews and ratings wield considerable influence over consumers' decisions and a business's online visibility:

- **Consumer Trust**: Reviews and ratings provide social proof, influencing potential customers' trust in a business. Positive reviews can encourage others to engage with your business.

- **Local SEO Impact**: Search engines like Google consider reviews and ratings as ranking factors, particularly in local search results. A business with a higher rating and a substantial number of reviews may outrank competitors.

- **User Engagement**: Reviews can lead to user engagement, as consumers often read and interact with reviews by asking questions or offering feedback.

- **Feedback and Improvement**: Constructive reviews can provide valuable insights for improving products or services and customer satisfaction.

2. Strategies for Garnering Positive Reviews

Encouraging customers to leave positive reviews is essential for your online reputation and local SEO:

a. Provide Exceptional Service: The foundation for positive reviews is exceptional customer service and quality products or services. Strive for excellence in every interaction.

b. Ask for Reviews: Don't hesitate to ask satisfied customers for reviews. You can include a polite request on your website, in email signatures, or during follow-up communication.

c. Make It Easy: Simplify the review process for customers by providing direct links to review platforms like Google, Yelp, or Facebook.

d. Timing Matters: Ask for reviews at the right time, such as immediately after a successful transaction or positive experience.

e. Respond to Reviews: Engage with customers who leave reviews, whether positive or negative. Responding shows that you value their feedback and can lead to more positive reviews.

f. Incentives: Consider offering small incentives or discounts for customers who leave reviews, but ensure compliance with review platform policies.

g. Monitor Reviews: Keep a close eye on review platforms and respond promptly to any negative feedback. Address concerns professionally and seek resolutions.

h. Showcase Positive Reviews: Feature positive reviews on your website, social media, or promotional materials to further build trust.

i. Encourage User-Generated Content: Encourage customers to share photos, videos, or stories about their experiences with your products or services, adding authenticity to your online presence.

j. Leverage Follow-Up Emails: Use follow-up emails to check in with customers and request reviews. Include direct links to make it convenient for them.

3. Managing Negative Reviews

Negative reviews are inevitable, but how you handle them can significantly impact your online reputation:

- **Respond Calmly**: Respond to negative reviews professionally and calmly. Avoid confrontations, and focus on resolving issues or providing additional information.

- **Apologize and Offer Solutions**: If a customer had a negative experience, offer a sincere apology and propose solutions to rectify the situation.

- **Take It Offline**: Whenever possible, move the conversation offline by providing contact information for further resolution.

- **Learn and Improve**: Use negative feedback as an opportunity for improvement. Address recurring issues and adjust your processes or offerings accordingly.

4. Guidelines for Online Reputation Management

Effective online reputation management involves more than just responding to reviews:

- **Monitor Constantly**: Regularly monitor review platforms, social media, and other online spaces for mentions of your business.

- **Be Consistent**: Ensure NAP consistency across all online platforms to build trust and credibility.

- **Encourage Positive Engagement**: Engage with your audience on social media, answer questions, and provide value to foster positive sentiment.

- **Educate Your Team**: Educate your team on the importance of online reputation management and proper response protocols.

- **Seek Professional Help**: For larger businesses or complex online reputation issues, consider consulting with professionals who specialize in reputation management.

5. The Influence of Ratings

Ratings (usually on a scale of 1 to 5 stars) are an essential aspect of reviews. They offer a quick way for consumers to assess a business's reputation:

- **5 Stars**: Excellent and highly recommended.

- **4 Stars**: Good with minor room for improvement.

- **3 Stars**: Average, with notable pros and cons.

- **2 Stars**: Below average with significant issues.

- **1 Star**: Poor experience, strongly discouraged.

Aim for high ratings by consistently delivering exceptional service and addressing customer concerns promptly.

In conclusion, customer reviews and ratings play a pivotal role in local SEO and online reputation management. Positive reviews enhance trust and visibility, while negative reviews present opportunities for improvement. By implementing strategies to encourage positive reviews, effectively managing negative feedback, and practicing good online reputation management, you can strengthen your online presence and foster a positive reputation that attracts and retains customers. As you explore these strategies in this section, you'll gain the knowledge and skills necessary to master customer reviews, ratings, and online reputation management for the benefit of your business's local SEO efforts.

E. Local SEO Ranking Factors

Local SEO ranking factors are the criteria that search engines use to determine the position of a business in local search results. In this section, we'll explore the key local SEO ranking factors, the role they play in local search rankings, and strategies for optimizing your business's online presence to improve local search visibility.

1. Google My Business Signals

Google My Business (GMB) is a foundational element of local SEO, and signals from your GMB listing heavily influence local search rankings:

• **Optimized GMB Profile**: Completing your GMB profile with accurate NAP information, categories, photos, and regular posts is crucial.

• **NAP Consistency**: Ensure that your business's Name, Address, and Phone number (NAP) are consistent across your GMB listing and other online platforms.

• **Verification**: Verify your GMB listing to confirm its authenticity.

• **Reviews and Ratings**: Encourage positive reviews and maintain a high rating on your GMB listing.

2. On-Page Signals

On-page signals refer to the content and structure of your website:

- **NAP on Website**: Include your business's NAP information on your website, ideally in the footer or contact page.

- **Localized Content**: Create high-quality, localized content that caters to your target audience's needs and interests.

- **Keyword Optimization**: Optimize your website's content for relevant local keywords, including city or neighborhood-specific terms.

- **Mobile-Friendly Design**: Ensure your website is mobile-friendly, as mobile users often conduct local searches.

- **Page Load Speed**: A fast-loading website improves user experience and can positively impact rankings.

3. Link Signals

Link signals include both the quantity and quality of backlinks to your website:

- **High-Quality Backlinks**: Earn high-quality backlinks from authoritative local websites, organizations, or directories.

- **Local Citations**: Citations from reputable local

directories and platforms can also positively impact local SEO.

4. On-Page Signals from GMB Landing Page

The landing page linked from your GMB listing plays a role in local search rankings:

- **Relevance**: Ensure the landing page is relevant to your business category and location.

- **Content Quality**: High-quality, informative content on the landing page can boost rankings.

- **Keyword Optimization**: Include relevant keywords and location-specific information.

5. Behavioral Signals

Behavioral signals reflect how users interact with your website and GMB listing:

- **Click-Through Rate (CTR)**: A high CTR indicates that users find your business appealing in search results.

- **User Engagement**: User engagement, including the time spent on your website, can affect rankings.

- **Mobile Click-to-Call**: Mobile users who click to call your business directly from search results send a positive signal.

6. Review Signals

Reviews and ratings influence local search rankings:

- **Review Quantity**: A greater number of reviews can positively impact rankings.

- **Review Velocity**: The pace at which you receive reviews also matters.

- **Review Diversity**: A mix of reviews (both in terms of sentiment and review sites) is beneficial.

7. Social Signals

Social signals refer to the activity and engagement on your social media profiles:

- **Active Profiles**: Maintain active and engaging social media profiles linked to your business.

- **Positive Engagement**: Encourage positive interactions and engagement with your social media content.

8. Google My Business Categories

Choose the most relevant categories for your business on your GMB listing. Accurate categorization can improve search result visibility.

9. Location Keywords in Anchor Text

If your business is mentioned in external content, having location-specific keywords in anchor text can boost local SEO.

10. Online Reputation

Your business's overall online reputation, which includes reviews and ratings on various platforms, can indirectly impact local search rankings.

11. Behavioral Data

Behavioral data, such as how users interact with your website and GMB listing, can inform search engines about your business's relevance and popularity.

12. Personalization

Search results may be personalized based on a user's location and search history.

13. Local Pack Rankings

The local pack, a prominent display of local businesses in search results, relies on several factors mentioned above, such as GMB signals, on-page signals, and review signals.

14. Competitive Landscape

The competitiveness of your local market and the actions of

your competitors can also influence your local SEO rankings.

In conclusion, local SEO ranking factors encompass a broad range of elements that search engines consider when determining the visibility of your business in local search results. By optimizing your Google My Business listing, fine-tuning your website, earning high-quality backlinks, encouraging positive reviews and engagement, and staying attuned to the local SEO landscape, you can enhance your business's local search visibility and attract more customers from your community. As you explore these strategies in this section, you'll gain the knowledge and skills necessary to master local SEO ranking factors for the benefit of your business's online presence.

Chapter 8:

Mobile SEO

Mobile SEO is a specialized discipline within the realm of search engine optimization that focuses on optimizing a website's visibility and performance in mobile search results. In this section, we'll delve into the world of Mobile SEO, exploring its significance, the unique challenges it presents, and the strategies necessary to ensure your website is mobile-friendly and primed for success in the era of mobile-first indexing. As mobile devices continue to dominate online interactions, understanding and mastering Mobile SEO is essential for businesses and webmasters seeking to thrive in the digital landscape.

A. Mobile-Friendly Design and Mobile-First Indexing

In today's digital age, the prevalence of smartphones and mobile devices has transformed the way people access information and conduct online activities. Mobile SEO is not just an option; it's a necessity. In this section, we will explore the critical aspects of mobile-friendly design and mobile-first indexing, both of which are fundamental to ensuring your website's success in the mobile era.

1. Mobile-Friendly Design

Mobile-friendly design, also known as responsive web design, is the practice of creating websites that provide an optimal user experience on a wide range of devices, including smartphones, tablets, and desktop computers. Here's why it's crucial:

- **User Experience**: Mobile users expect websites to load quickly and display correctly on their devices. A mobile-friendly design ensures a seamless and satisfying user experience.

- **SEO Rankings**: Google and other search engines prioritize mobile-friendly websites in mobile search results. A mobile-friendly design can positively impact your search rankings.

Key Elements of Mobile-Friendly Design:

a. Responsive Layout: The design should adapt fluidly to various screen sizes and orientations, eliminating the need for horizontal scrolling or zooming.

b. Fast Page Load Speed: Optimize images and code to ensure rapid page load times, a critical factor for mobile users.

c. Mobile Navigation: Implement mobile-friendly navigation menus, such as hamburger menus or simplified navigation structures.

d. Readability: Use legible fonts and appropriate text sizes to enhance readability on smaller screens.

e. Touch-Friendly Buttons: Ensure that interactive elements like buttons and links are large enough to tap easily on touchscreens.

f. Content Prioritization: Prioritize content and consider mobile-specific content strategies, such as collapsible sections for longer articles.

g. Avoid Flash: Avoid technologies like Flash that are not supported on many mobile devices.

h. Test on Real Devices: Regularly test your website on actual mobile devices to identify and address any usability issues.

2. Mobile-First Indexing

Mobile-first indexing is a significant shift in how Google and other search engines crawl, index, and rank websites. With mobile-first indexing, the mobile version of a website becomes the primary version for indexing and ranking. Here's what you need to know:

- **Mobile-First Priority**: Google primarily uses the mobile version of a website for ranking and indexing. If your website isn't mobile-friendly, it may negatively impact your search rankings.

Key Considerations for Mobile-First Indexing:

a. Mobile Version Parity: Ensure that the content and metadata on your mobile version are equivalent to the desktop version. Missing content on mobile can affect rankings.

b. Structured Data: Implement structured data markup (schema markup) on your mobile site to provide context to search engines.

c. Mobile Sitemaps: Create and submit a mobile sitemap to Google to help it discover and index your mobile content.

d. Page Speed: Optimize your mobile site for fast page load speeds, as this is a ranking factor for mobile search.

e. Responsive Design: A responsive design is Google's recommended approach for mobile-friendly websites.

f. Avoid Separate Mobile Sites: While separate mobile sites were once popular, they can introduce complexities in indexing. Google recommends using responsive design or dynamic serving instead.

g. Mobile User Experience: Continuously monitor and enhance the user experience on your mobile site, as user engagement signals can impact rankings.

In conclusion, mobile-friendly design and mobile-first

indexing are inseparable in today's SEO landscape. A mobile-friendly website is essential for providing a positive user experience and for maintaining or improving your search rankings. As mobile device usage continues to rise, mastering these aspects of Mobile SEO is critical to ensuring your website's success in reaching and engaging with mobile users effectively. By implementing responsive design, optimizing your mobile site for speed and user experience, and staying informed about mobile-first indexing, you'll be well-equipped to thrive in the mobile-centric digital world.

B. Mobile Page Speed and Accelerated Mobile Pages (AMP)

Mobile page speed is not just a convenience; it's a critical factor in Mobile SEO and user experience. Additionally, Accelerated Mobile Pages (AMP) is a technology that can significantly enhance the speed and performance of mobile web pages. In this section, we will delve into the importance of mobile page speed, discuss strategies for optimizing it, and explore the role of AMP in mobile SEO.

1. Importance of Mobile Page Speed

Mobile page speed, which refers to how quickly a web page loads on a mobile device, is vital for several reasons:

- **User Experience**: Users expect websites to load quickly on mobile devices. Slow-loading pages frustrate users and increase bounce rates.

- **SEO Rankings**: Google considers page speed as a ranking factor in its algorithm, especially for mobile search results. Faster-loading pages are more likely to rank higher.

- **Conversion Rates**: Faster page speeds can lead to higher conversion rates and better user engagement.

2. Strategies for Improving Mobile Page Speed

Optimizing mobile page speed involves a combination of technical and content-related strategies:

a. Image Optimization: Compress and optimize images to reduce their file sizes while maintaining quality. Use responsive images to ensure they adapt to different screen sizes.

b. Minimize HTTP Requests: Reduce the number of HTTP requests by combining CSS and JavaScript files and minimizing unnecessary resources.

c. Browser Caching: Implement browser caching to store elements of your website locally on the user's device, reducing the need to re-download resources on subsequent visits.

d. Content Delivery Networks (CDNs): Use CDNs to

distribute website content across multiple servers, improving load times for users in different geographic locations.

e. Minimize Redirects: Minimize the use of redirects, as they can slow down page loading. Ensure that any redirects are necessary and optimized.

f. Enable Browser Compression: Enable GZIP or Brotli compression to reduce the size of HTML, CSS, and JavaScript files sent to the user's device.

g. Prioritize Above-the-Fold Content: Load critical content (above-the-fold) first to provide users with a faster initial experience.

h. Reduce Server Response Time: Optimize server response times by using efficient hosting and server configurations.

i. AMP Implementation: Consider implementing Accelerated Mobile Pages (AMP) for select pages, especially content-heavy pages like articles and blogs.

j. Limit Third-Party Scripts: Minimize the use of third-party scripts and widgets, as they can introduce additional overhead.

k. Monitor Performance: Regularly monitor your website's mobile performance using tools like Google PageSpeed Insights or Lighthouse. Address any issues or recommendations promptly.

3. Accelerated Mobile Pages (AMP)

Accelerated Mobile Pages (AMP) is an open-source initiative designed to create faster-loading web pages for mobile users. Key aspects of AMP include:

- **Stripped-Down HTML**: AMP pages use a simplified version of HTML, which prioritizes performance and speed. Certain HTML tags and attributes are restricted to improve load times.

- **Caching**: Google caches AMP pages on its servers, enabling near-instant loading when users access these pages from search results.

- **Limited JavaScript**: AMP restricts the use of JavaScript, allowing only asynchronous scripts and enforcing certain best practices to prevent performance bottlenecks.

- **Optimized CSS**: CSS in AMP is designed to be streamlined and efficient, enhancing rendering speed.

- **Analytics Support**: AMP allows for the integration of analytics and tracking, ensuring that businesses can gather data on user engagement.

4. Implementing AMP

To implement AMP on your website:

- Create separate AMP versions of your web pages using AMP HTML and AMP JavaScript components.

- Add structured data markup (schema markup) to your AMP pages to provide context to search engines.

- Submit your AMP pages to Google for indexing.

- Monitor and maintain your AMP pages to ensure they continue to meet the AMP standards.

5. Balancing AMP and Mobile Page Speed Optimization

While AMP can significantly enhance mobile page speed, it's not necessary for every page on your website. Reserve AMP for content-heavy pages like articles and blogs where faster loading times are critical. For other pages, continue optimizing for mobile page speed using the strategies mentioned earlier.

In conclusion, mobile page speed is paramount for both user satisfaction and SEO rankings in the mobile-centric digital landscape. By optimizing your website for speed, minimizing page load times, and considering the implementation of Accelerated Mobile Pages (AMP) where appropriate, you can provide an exceptional mobile user experience and improve your website's visibility in mobile search results. As you explore these strategies in this section, you'll gain the knowledge and skills necessary to master mobile page speed and AMP implementation for the benefit of your Mobile SEO efforts.

C. App Indexing and Mobile SEO Best Practices

As mobile devices continue to dominate online interactions, App Indexing and Mobile SEO play a pivotal role in enhancing user experience and visibility in mobile search results. In this section, we will explore the significance of App Indexing, delve into Mobile SEO best practices, and provide guidance on optimizing your mobile app's presence for both search engines and users.

1. Significance of App Indexing

App Indexing, also known as App Deep Linking, is the process of making the content within a mobile app discoverable and accessible through search engines. It bridges the gap between mobile apps and traditional web search. Here's why App Indexing is crucial:

• **Enhanced User Experience**: App Indexing allows users to seamlessly transition between web content and app content, improving the overall user experience.

• **Increased App Engagement**: When users discover app content through search results, they are more likely to engage with and use the app.

- **SEO Benefits**: App Indexing can positively impact your mobile app's visibility in search engine results, potentially increasing app downloads and usage.

2. Mobile SEO Best Practices

Effective Mobile SEO requires attention to detail, especially in a mobile-first world. Here are some best practices to optimize your mobile web presence:

a. Mobile-Friendly Design: Ensure that your website is responsive and provides an excellent user experience on mobile devices.

b. Page Load Speed: Optimize your mobile site for fast page load times. Mobile users have little patience for slow-loading pages.

c. Mobile SEO Audit: Regularly perform mobile SEO audits to identify and address issues that may impact your mobile site's performance and ranking.

d. Mobile-Friendly Content: Craft mobile-friendly content that is concise, easy to read, and formatted for mobile screens.

e. Local SEO Optimization: If your business has a physical presence, prioritize local SEO optimization for mobile users, including accurate NAP (Name, Address, Phone) information.

f. Structured Data Markup: Implement structured data markup (schema markup) to provide context to search engines and improve the visibility of your content.

g. Voice Search Optimization: As voice search grows in popularity on mobile devices, optimize your content for natural language queries.

h. Mobile Sitemaps: Create and submit a mobile sitemap to help search engines discover and index your mobile content effectively.

i. Mobile Usability: Prioritize mobile usability by ensuring that buttons and interactive elements are touch-friendly and well-spaced.

3. App Indexing Best Practices

App Indexing enhances the discoverability of your mobile app content in search results. Here are some best practices:

a. Create App Deep Links: Implement deep links in your app to specific content pages, enabling search engines to index and link to app content.

b. App Indexing API: Utilize the App Indexing API provided by Google (or platform-specific alternatives) to communicate with search engines about your app's content.

c. Verify Ownership: Verify ownership of your app in Google Search Console to access App Indexing tools and data.

d. Maintain Content Parity: Ensure that content within your app is equivalent to that on your website. Content parity is critical for consistent user experiences.

e. Provide High-Quality App Content: Offer high-quality content within your app to encourage user engagement and positive reviews.

f. Monitor App Indexing Errors: Regularly monitor for app indexing errors and address them promptly to maintain indexing and ranking.

4. Promote Your App: Encourage users to download and use your app through your website, email campaigns, and social media channels. Increased app downloads can improve app visibility in search results.

5. App Store Optimization (ASO): Optimize your app's listing in app stores (e.g., Google Play Store, Apple App Store) with relevant keywords, engaging descriptions, and appealing visuals.

6. User Reviews and Ratings: Encourage users to leave positive reviews and ratings for your app, as these can impact app store rankings.

7. User Engagement: Focus on user engagement within your app, as factors like app usage, session duration, and user interactions can indirectly influence app store rankings.

In conclusion, App Indexing and Mobile SEO are integral components of digital marketing in the mobile age. By implementing best practices for mobile web optimization, ensuring content consistency across web and app, and following guidelines for app indexing, you can enhance the visibility of your mobile app in search results and provide a seamless experience for mobile users. As you explore these strategies in this section, you'll gain the knowledge and skills necessary to master App Indexing and Mobile SEO, contributing to the success of your mobile app and web presence.

D. Voice Search Optimization

As voice-activated digital assistants and smart speakers become increasingly prevalent, voice search optimization has become a crucial aspect of mobile SEO. In this section, we'll explore the significance of voice search, the unique challenges it presents, and the strategies for optimizing your web content to excel in voice search results.

1. The Significance of Voice Search

Voice search is fundamentally changing how users interact

with search engines, especially on mobile devices. Here's why voice search is significant:

- **Rising Popularity**: Voice-activated devices like smartphones, smart speakers (e.g., Amazon Echo, Google Home), and voice assistants (e.g., Siri, Google Assistant) are growing in popularity.

- **Convenience**: Voice search is faster and more convenient than typing, especially on mobile devices. Users can simply speak their queries.

- **Natural Language**: Users tend to use more conversational, long-tail queries in voice search, making it distinct from text-based search.

- **Local Searches**: Many voice searches are location-specific ("Where's the nearest coffee shop?"), making it crucial for businesses with physical locations.

2. Voice Search Optimization Strategies

Optimizing for voice search involves tailoring your content and SEO efforts to match the way people speak and interact with voice-activated devices. Here are key strategies:

a. Natural Language Keywords: Focus on long-tail and conversational keywords that mimic how people speak. Instead of "best pizza NYC," think "Where can I find the best pizza in New

York City?"

b. FAQ Content: Create content that answers common questions related to your industry, products, or services. FAQs are rich in natural language queries.

c. Schema Markup: Implement structured data markup (schema markup) to provide context to search engines and improve the chances of your content appearing in featured snippets or voice search results.

d. Mobile Optimization: Ensure your website is mobile-friendly and loads quickly, as voice searches often occur on mobile devices.

e. Local SEO: Optimize for local voice searches by providing accurate NAP (Name, Address, Phone) information, claiming your Google My Business listing, and encouraging user reviews.

f. Featured Snippets: Aim to secure featured snippet positions, as voice search often sources answers from these concise, high-ranking snippets.

g. Page Speed: Optimize your website for fast loading times, as voice assistants prefer delivering quick results.

h. Voice Search Queries Analysis: Analyze voice search queries to understand user intent and tailor your content accordingly.

i. Natural Content: Create content that sounds conversational and human rather than overly formal. Voice search results often reflect a natural tone.

j. Mobile App Integration: If you have a mobile app, consider integrating it with voice assistants to provide users with app-based voice search capabilities.

k. Test Voice Search Performance: Regularly test how your website and content perform in voice search results on different devices and platforms.

l. Voice Search-Specific Pages: Develop content specifically tailored to voice search queries, including "How-to" guides, tutorials, and quick answers.

3. Voice Search Challenges

Optimizing for voice search comes with its challenges:

- **Lack of Visuals**: Voice search relies purely on audio responses, so there are no visual elements like search engine results pages (SERPs). Optimizing for voice means aiming for featured snippets and position zero.

- **Query Length**: Voice searches tend to be longer and more conversational, requiring a different approach to keyword research and content optimization.

- **Local Competition**: Local businesses face competition for voice searches with other nearby businesses. Accurate NAP information and strong local SEO are crucial.

- **Device-Specific Optimization**: Voice search can vary depending on the device and virtual assistant used (e.g., Siri, Google Assistant, Alexa), requiring adaptation to multiple platforms.

- **Privacy Concerns**: Users may have privacy concerns related to voice search, which could affect adoption rates.

In conclusion, voice search optimization is an evolving field that necessitates adapting to changing user behavior and technology trends. As voice-activated devices continue to proliferate, mastering voice search optimization is crucial for staying competitive in mobile SEO. By focusing on natural language, featured snippets, local SEO, and mobile optimization, you can improve your website's visibility in voice search results and provide users with the valuable, conversational information they seek. As you explore these strategies in this section, you'll gain the knowledge and skills necessary to excel in the world of voice search optimization.

E. Mobile SEO Testing and Analysis

Testing and analysis are essential components of any

successful SEO strategy, and this holds true for Mobile SEO as well. In this section, we will explore the importance of mobile SEO testing and analysis, the key areas to focus on, and the tools and techniques that can help you optimize your mobile web presence effectively.

1. Significance of Mobile SEO Testing and Analysis

Mobile SEO testing and analysis are crucial for several reasons:

• **User Experience**: Mobile users have unique preferences and behaviors, so testing helps ensure that your website provides an optimal experience on various mobile devices and screen sizes.

• **SEO Performance**: Monitoring and analyzing mobile SEO performance allows you to identify issues, track improvements, and maintain or improve your mobile search rankings.

• **Algorithm Changes**: Search engines regularly update their algorithms, and mobile-specific changes can impact your rankings. Testing helps you adapt to these changes.

• **Competitive Advantage**: By continuously testing and optimizing your mobile site, you can gain a competitive advantage by staying ahead of your competitors in mobile search results.

2. Key Areas of Mobile SEO Testing

When conducting mobile SEO testing, focus on the following key areas:

a. Mobile-Friendly Design: Ensure that your website is responsive and provides an excellent user experience on various mobile devices, including smartphones and tablets.

b. Page Load Speed: Test your mobile site's load times to identify and resolve any issues that may affect performance.

c. Mobile Usability: Evaluate the usability of your mobile site, including navigation, touch-friendly elements, and overall user-friendliness.

d. Content Presentation: Ensure that your content is well-structured and easy to read on smaller screens. Test how content flows and appears on mobile devices.

e. Mobile SEO Audit: Regularly perform comprehensive mobile SEO audits to identify technical issues, broken links, and other SEO-related problems.

f. Mobile Keyword Optimization: Test how your chosen keywords perform on mobile devices and make adjustments as needed.

g. Mobile Local SEO: Verify the accuracy of your local SEO efforts, including NAP (Name, Address, Phone) information, on mobile devices.

h. Mobile Schema Markup: Test structured data markup (schema markup) to ensure that it displays correctly on mobile devices.

i. Mobile Analytics: Monitor mobile-specific analytics to track user behavior, conversions, and engagement on your mobile site.

j. Voice Search Testing: If applicable, analyze how your website performs in voice search results and make adjustments accordingly.

3. Mobile SEO Testing Tools and Techniques

To effectively conduct mobile SEO testing and analysis, you can use a combination of tools and techniques:

a. Google's Mobile-Friendly Test: Google provides a free tool that assesses the mobile-friendliness of your website and provides recommendations for improvement.

b. PageSpeed Insights: Google's PageSpeed Insights tool offers insights into your mobile site's performance and suggests optimizations.

c. Mobile Emulators: Use mobile emulators or device simulators to test how your site appears and functions on various mobile devices.

d. Mobile Usability Reports: Google Search Console provides mobile usability reports, highlighting issues that may negatively impact mobile user experience.

e. Mobile SEO Auditing Tools: Tools like Screaming Frog and SEMrush offer mobile SEO auditing features to identify technical issues and areas for improvement.

f. Mobile Analytics: Leverage mobile-specific analytics tools, such as Google Analytics, to track user behavior, conversions, and mobile-specific metrics.

g. User Testing: Conduct usability testing with real users on mobile devices to gather feedback and identify issues from a user perspective.

h. A/B Testing: Run A/B tests on mobile pages to compare different versions and determine which elements or changes lead to better mobile performance.

i. Mobile-Friendly Test Data: Analyze data from Google's Mobile-Friendly Test to assess improvements and track your mobile SEO progress over time.

j. Competitive Analysis: Study how your competitors perform in mobile search results and identify strategies they may be using.

4. Regular Monitoring and Iteration

Mobile SEO testing and analysis are not one-time activities; they should be ongoing processes. Regularly monitor your mobile site's performance, track changes in mobile search rankings, and adapt your strategies based on the data you gather. SEO is dynamic, and the mobile landscape evolves, so continuous testing and optimization are essential for long-term success.

In conclusion, mobile SEO testing and analysis are fundamental to maintaining and improving your mobile web presence. By focusing on mobile-friendly design, page speed, usability, content presentation, and other key areas, and by utilizing the right tools and techniques, you can ensure that your mobile site not only meets user expectations but also ranks well in mobile search results. As you explore these strategies in this section, you'll gain the knowledge and skills necessary to excel in mobile SEO testing and analysis, ultimately contributing to the success of your mobile SEO efforts.

Chapter 9:

SEO Analytics and Reporting

In the ever-evolving landscape of digital marketing, the ability to measure, analyze, and report on your SEO efforts is paramount to achieving success. This section explores the world of SEO analytics and reporting, offering insights into the importance of data-driven decision-making, the key metrics and tools involved, and how to effectively communicate your SEO performance to stakeholders and clients. Whether you're a seasoned SEO professional or just embarking on your SEO journey, understanding SEO analytics and reporting is essential for optimizing your online presence and achieving your digital marketing goals.

A. Setting Up Google Analytics

Google Analytics is a powerful tool that provides valuable insights into your website's performance, user behavior, and the effectiveness of your SEO efforts. Setting up Google Analytics correctly is the first step toward harnessing this wealth of data. In this section, we will delve into the process of setting up Google Analytics, including creating an account, installing tracking code, and configuring essential settings.

1. Create a Google Analytics Account

a. Sign In or Create a Google Account: If you already have a Google account, sign in. If not, create one by visiting the Google Analytics website and clicking "Start for free."

b. Set Up Your Google Analytics Property: After signing in, click on "Start measuring" and follow the prompts to create your first property. A property represents your website or app.

c. Configure Property Details: Provide information about your website, including its name, URL, industry category, and reporting time zone. Review and accept the terms of service.

d. Data Sharing Settings: Google may ask for your data-sharing preferences. Review these options and make selections based on your preferences.

2. Get Your Tracking Code

Once you've created a property, Google Analytics will provide you with a unique tracking code. This code is essential for collecting data from your website. Follow these steps to obtain your tracking code:

a. Accept the Tracking Code Terms: After creating a property, you'll be presented with a tracking code snippet and a set of terms. Review and accept the terms.

b. Install the Tracking Code: Copy the tracking code snippet provided by Google Analytics. It typically looks like a block of JavaScript code.

c. Paste the Tracking Code on Your Website: Paste the tracking code into the HTML of your website's pages, just before the closing </head> tag. You need to do this for every page on your website to ensure comprehensive data collection.

d. Verify Tracking Code Installation: Google Analytics provides a real-time tracking feature that allows you to verify if the tracking code is working correctly. You can do this by accessing the "Realtime" reports in your Google Analytics account.

3. Configure Essential Settings

After setting up your tracking code, there are several essential settings to configure within your Google Analytics account:

a. Goals and E-commerce Tracking: If your website has specific goals like form submissions, downloads, or e-commerce transactions, configure goals and e-commerce tracking to measure and report on these important actions.

b. Site Search Tracking: If your website includes an internal search feature, enable site search tracking to gain insights into what users are searching for on your site.

c. Filters and Views: Set up filters and create different views to segment your data based on specific criteria, such as excluding internal traffic or tracking subdomains separately.

d. Annotations: Use annotations to document significant events or changes on your website. Annotations help provide context when analyzing data.

e. Custom Alerts: Configure custom alerts to receive notifications when unusual or critical changes occur in your data, such as sudden traffic drops.

f. Referral Exclusion List: Prevent self-referrals by adding your domain to the referral exclusion list. This ensures that your data accurately reflects user interactions on your site.

g. Channel Groupings: Customize channel groupings to categorize traffic sources according to your business needs.

h. Mobile App Tracking: If you have a mobile app, set up mobile app tracking to collect data on app usage and user engagement.

i. Data Retention: Determine how long you want Google Analytics to retain your data. Choose the retention period that aligns with your reporting and analysis needs.

4. Verify Data Collection

After configuring these settings, it's crucial to verify that data is being collected accurately. To do this, navigate through your Google Analytics reports and ensure that data is appearing as expected. Pay attention to key metrics like website traffic, user behavior, and conversions.

5. Set Up Goals and Conversions

To measure the effectiveness of your SEO efforts, set up goals and conversions that align with your business objectives. Common goals include form submissions, e-commerce transactions, newsletter sign-ups, and more. By tracking these goals, you can assess the impact of your SEO strategy on driving desired actions.

In conclusion, setting up Google Analytics is a foundational step in SEO analytics and reporting. By creating an account, installing the tracking code, configuring essential settings, and verifying data collection, you lay the groundwork for data-driven decision-making. Accurate and comprehensive data collection is essential for assessing the impact of your SEO efforts, identifying areas for improvement, and optimizing your website's performance. As you explore these steps in this section, you'll gain the knowledge and skills necessary to set up Google Analytics effectively and leverage its insights to enhance your SEO strategy.

B. SEO Performance Metrics (Traffic, Rankings, Conversions)

Evaluating the performance of your SEO efforts is essential to understanding the effectiveness of your strategy and making informed decisions. In this section, we will explore key SEO performance metrics, including website traffic, rankings, and conversions. Understanding and analyzing these metrics will empower you to assess the impact of your SEO initiatives and optimize your digital presence for better results.

1. Website Traffic Metrics

a. Organic Traffic: Organic traffic refers to the number of visitors who arrive at your website through organic search results. This metric is a fundamental indicator of your SEO performance. Analyze organic traffic trends over time to assess the impact of your SEO efforts.

b. Total Traffic: Total traffic encompasses all visitors to your website, including organic, direct, referral, and paid traffic sources. Understanding the overall traffic volume provides context for your SEO efforts.

c. Traffic Sources: Dive deeper into traffic sources to identify where your visitors are coming from. Analyze the proportion of traffic from organic search, direct visits, referrals, social media, and paid campaigns.

d. Bounce Rate: Bounce rate measures the percentage of visitors who leave your site after viewing only one page. A high bounce rate may indicate issues with content quality or user experience.

e. Session Duration: Session duration reflects the average amount of time users spend on your site. Longer sessions often indicate engaging content and a positive user experience.

f. Pages per Session: This metric shows the average number of pages viewed during a single session. Higher page per session numbers suggest that users are exploring your site's content.

g. New vs. Returning Visitors: Distinguish between new and returning visitors to understand user engagement and the ability to retain an audience.

2. Ranking Metrics

a. Keyword Rankings: Track the rankings of your target keywords in search engine results pages (SERPs). Monitor rankings for specific keywords and assess changes over time.

b. SERP Visibility: Calculate your website's visibility in SERPs by considering the rankings of multiple keywords. Tools like the Search Visibility Index can provide a comprehensive view of your site's presence in search results.

c. Click-Through Rate (CTR): CTR measures the percentage of users who click on your website's link in search results. A higher CTR indicates that your page's title and meta description are compelling.

d. Impressions: Impressions represent how often your website appears in search results. An increase in impressions suggests improved visibility.

e. Clicks: Analyze the total number of clicks your website receives from search results. Tracking clicks alongside impressions and CTR provides a more comprehensive view of user engagement.

f. Featured Snippets and Position Zero: If your content appears in featured snippets or the coveted position zero in SERPs, monitor this metric as it can significantly impact visibility and click-through rates.

3. Conversion Metrics

a. Goal Completions: Set up goals in Google Analytics to track specific user actions, such as form submissions, newsletter sign-ups, or e-commerce transactions. Measure the number of goal completions tied to your SEO efforts.

b. Conversion Rate: Conversion rate calculates the percentage of visitors who complete a predefined goal. It reflects the effectiveness of your site in converting visitors into leads or customers.

c. Revenue from SEO: For e-commerce websites, track the revenue generated from SEO-driven conversions. Assess the ROI of your SEO strategy by comparing revenue to SEO investment.

d. Assisted Conversions: Explore the role of SEO in the user's journey. Assisted conversions indicate how often SEO contributes to conversions, even if it's not the last touchpoint.

e. Conversion Funnel Analysis: Examine the steps users take before completing a conversion. Identify potential bottlenecks or areas for improvement in the conversion process.

f. Return on Investment (ROI): Calculate the ROI of your SEO efforts by comparing the revenue generated from SEO to the costs associated with SEO campaigns, including content creation, link building, and optimization.

4. User Behavior Metrics

a. Pageviews: Track the number of pageviews to understand which pages are popular among users.

b. Exit Pages: Identify the pages where users most commonly exit your site. Optimize these pages to encourage users to explore further.

c. User Engagement: Monitor user engagement metrics like comments, social shares, and time spent on page to gauge content quality and audience interaction.

d. Mobile Performance: Analyze mobile-specific metrics, such as mobile bounce rate and mobile conversion rate, to ensure your site is mobile-friendly and responsive.

e. Site Speed Metrics: Assess site speed metrics, including page load times and server response times, to optimize the user experience.

In conclusion, SEO performance metrics are vital for assessing the impact of your SEO strategy and making data-driven decisions. By monitoring website traffic, rankings, conversions, and user behavior, you can gain valuable insights into your SEO efforts' effectiveness and make adjustments to optimize your digital presence. As you explore these metrics in this section, you'll gain the knowledge and skills necessary to measure and report on your SEO performance comprehensively.

C. SEO Reporting Tools and Dashboards

Efficient reporting is a critical component of successful SEO management. It allows you to communicate your SEO progress, demonstrate the impact of your efforts, and make data-driven decisions. In this section, we'll delve into the world of SEO reporting tools and dashboards, exploring the essential tools, best practices, and key elements for creating insightful reports.

1. Importance of SEO Reporting

Effective SEO reporting serves several essential purposes:

- **Performance Assessment**: Reports provide a comprehensive view of your SEO efforts, helping you evaluate their effectiveness and identify areas for improvement.

- **Communication**: Reports facilitate communication with clients, stakeholders, and team members, helping them understand the value of SEO initiatives.

- **Data-Driven Decisions**: Data presented in reports inform decision-making, enabling you to adjust strategies, allocate resources, and set priorities based on evidence.

2. Key Elements of SEO Reports

To create informative SEO reports, consider including these key elements:

a. Executive Summary: A concise overview of the report's findings, including high-level metrics and highlights.

b. Goals and Objectives: Clearly state the goals and objectives of the SEO campaign to provide context for the report.

c. Key Performance Indicators (KPIs): Highlight relevant

KPIs, such as organic traffic growth, keyword rankings, conversion rates, and ROI, to showcase progress.

d. Traffic and Ranking Data: Present data on website traffic, including organic, direct, and referral traffic, as well as keyword rankings.

e. Conversion and Goal Data: Include information on conversions and goal completions, tying them back to SEO efforts.

f. Content Performance: Analyze the performance of specific content pieces, such as blog posts or landing pages, highlighting top-performing content.

g. Link Building and Backlinks: Report on link-building activities, the acquisition of high-quality backlinks, and the impact on SEO.

h. Technical SEO Audit: Summarize the results of technical SEO audits, listing identified issues and the status of resolutions.

i. Competitor Analysis: Include insights from competitor analysis, highlighting areas where your website can gain a competitive edge.

j. Recommendations: Provide actionable recommendations for ongoing SEO improvement based on data analysis.

k. Visualizations: Incorporate charts, graphs, and visual representations of data to make the report more engaging and understandable.

l. Historical Data: Compare current data with historical data to demonstrate progress over time.

3. SEO Reporting Tools

Several tools can help streamline the process of creating SEO reports and dashboards:

a. Google Analytics: Google Analytics offers customizable reporting options and integration with other Google services like Google Data Studio.

b. Google Data Studio: A free tool that allows you to create interactive and customizable data dashboards, including SEO-specific reports.

c. SEO Reporting Software: Tools like Moz, SEMrush, Ahrefs, and Raven Tools provide SEO reporting features, making it easier to gather and visualize data.

d. Microsoft Excel and Google Sheets: These spreadsheet tools enable you to create custom reports by importing data from various sources.

e. SEO Plugins: If you're using a content management system

(CMS) like WordPress, consider SEO plugins that offer reporting features.

f. Custom Development: For advanced reporting needs, consider custom development solutions tailored to your specific requirements.

4. Best Practices for SEO Reporting

When creating SEO reports, follow these best practices:

a. Set Clear Objectives: Define the purpose and objectives of the report to ensure that it provides actionable insights.

b. Tailor Reports to the Audience: Customize reports for different audiences, whether they are executives, clients, or internal team members. Focus on presenting information that is relevant to their needs and understanding.

c. Use Visuals: Visual elements like charts, graphs, and tables can help simplify complex data and make it more digestible.

d. Explain Trends: Interpret the data and trends in the report, providing context and explanations for fluctuations or changes.

e. Highlight Achievements: Celebrate successes and achievements, showcasing how SEO efforts have positively impacted the business.

f. Include Actionable Recommendations: Offer specific,

actionable recommendations based on the data presented in the report.

g. Regular Reporting Schedule: Establish a regular reporting schedule to keep stakeholders informed and engaged.

h. Share Insights: Beyond data, share insights and explanations of what the data means for the business.

i. Encourage Collaboration: Use reports as a tool to foster collaboration and discussions about SEO strategies.

5. Continuous Improvement

SEO reporting is not a static process. Regularly review your reporting process and templates to ensure they align with evolving business goals and SEO strategies. Seek feedback from stakeholders to make improvements and refine your reporting approach over time.

In conclusion, SEO reporting tools and dashboards are essential for evaluating the impact of your SEO efforts, communicating progress to stakeholders, and making data-driven decisions. By following best practices, customizing reports to your audience's needs, and leveraging reporting tools, you can create informative and insightful SEO reports that drive improved SEO strategies and results. As you explore these tools and practices in this section, you'll gain the knowledge and skills necessary to excel in the realm of SEO reporting.

D. A/B Testing and Experimentation

A/B testing and experimentation are powerful tools in the SEO toolkit, allowing you to make data-driven decisions, optimize your website, and improve user experience. In this section, we'll explore the principles, methodologies, and best practices for A/B testing and experimentation in the context of SEO.

1. Understanding A/B Testing

A/B testing, also known as split testing, is a method of comparing two versions of a webpage or element (A and B) to determine which one performs better in achieving a specific goal. In the context of SEO, A/B testing helps you assess changes in elements like content, design, or layout to determine their impact on search rankings and user engagement.

2. A/B Testing Process

A successful A/B testing process involves several key steps:

a. Hypothesis: Start by forming a clear hypothesis about what you want to test and the expected impact of the change. For example, you might hypothesize that changing the meta description of a page will lead to a higher click-through rate (CTR).

b. Variations: Create two versions (A and B) of the element you're testing. One version remains unchanged (control), while the other incorporates the proposed change (variant).

c. Random Assignment: Randomly assign users to either the control group (A) or the variant group (B) when they visit your webpage. This ensures unbiased results.

d. Data Collection: Collect data on user interactions, such as click-through rates, conversion rates, bounce rates, and other relevant metrics.

e. Statistical Analysis: Analyze the data to determine whether there is a statistically significant difference between the control and variant groups. Tools like Google Optimize or Optimizely can assist with this analysis.

f. Decision Making: Based on the analysis, decide whether to implement the change (variant B) or stick with the original (control A).

g. Implementation: If the variant outperforms the control, implement the change on your website. If not, discard the variant and consider other hypotheses.

3. Common A/B Testing Scenarios in SEO

a. Title Tags and Meta Descriptions: Test different title tags and meta descriptions to see which ones result in higher click-through rates from search engine results pages (SERPs).

b. Content Variations: Experiment with different content layouts, headings, and styles to determine which format engages users better.

c. Call-to-Action (CTA) Buttons: Test variations of CTA buttons, such as color, text, and placement, to see which ones lead to more conversions.

d. Page Load Times: Optimize page load times to improve user experience and reduce bounce rates.

e. Mobile-Friendly Design: Test mobile-friendly design changes to enhance the mobile user experience and potentially improve mobile search rankings.

f. Structured Data Markup: Experiment with structured data markup to enhance how your website appears in search results, potentially increasing click-through rates.

4. SEO Experimentation

In addition to traditional A/B testing, SEO experimentation involves systematic testing of SEO strategies and changes over time. SEO experimentation focuses on optimizing for search engine visibility and user experience. Key principles of SEO experimentation include:

a. Controlled Environment: Ensure that your experiments are conducted in a controlled environment to isolate the impact of specific SEO changes.

b. Long-term Analysis: Some SEO changes may take time to yield results. Therefore, SEO experimentation often involves long-term analysis to measure the effects accurately.

c. Measurement Tools: Use SEO measurement tools and analytics platforms to track changes in organic traffic, keyword rankings, and user engagement.

d. Tracking Algorithm Updates: Keep an eye on search engine algorithm updates and assess their impact on your website's performance. Adapt your SEO strategy as needed.

e. User Experience: Consider how SEO changes affect user experience, as user engagement is a crucial factor in search engine rankings.

f. Data-Driven Decision-Making: Base SEO strategy adjustments on data-driven insights gained from experimentation.

5. SEO Experimentation Tools

To conduct SEO experimentation effectively, consider using tools like:

a. Google Search Console: Monitor keyword rankings,

impressions, click-through rates, and other performance metrics.

b. Google Analytics: Track user behavior, conversions, and engagement on your website.

c. SEO Testing Tools: Tools like DistilledODN and RankSense are specifically designed for SEO experimentation and testing.

d. Data Analysis Tools: Excel, Google Sheets, and data visualization tools like Tableau can help you analyze the results of your experiments.

6. Best Practices

a. Start Small: Begin with small-scale experiments to refine your process and gain experience.

b. Monitor Trends: Pay attention to industry trends and algorithm updates, as they can impact the results of your SEO experiments.

c. Maintain a Control Group: Always have a control group to compare against the experimental group.

d. Document Everything: Keep detailed records of your experiments, including the changes made, the rationale behind them, and the results.

e. Be Patient: SEO experimentation may not yield immediate results. Be patient and allow experiments to run for an appropriate duration.

7. Continuous Improvement

SEO is an ever-evolving field, and experimentation is a key component of staying ahead of the curve. Continuously refine your SEO experimentation process and adapt your strategies based on the insights gained from testing.

In conclusion, A/B testing and SEO experimentation are essential tools for improving SEO performance, user experience, and website rankings. By following the principles and best practices outlined in this section, you can systematically test and optimize your website's elements and SEO strategies, leading to better results and a stronger online presence.

E. SEO ROI and Measuring Success

Measuring the return on investment (ROI) of your SEO efforts is crucial for assessing the effectiveness of your strategies and demonstrating their value to stakeholders. In this section, we'll delve into the intricacies of SEO ROI and how to accurately measure success in the context of search engine optimization.

1. Understanding SEO ROI

SEO ROI is a measurement of the return on investment for your search engine optimization efforts. It quantifies the value generated from your SEO activities in relation to the costs incurred. A positive ROI indicates that your SEO efforts are generating more value than they cost, while a negative ROI suggests the opposite.

2. Calculating SEO ROI

To calculate SEO ROI, you'll need to consider both the returns (benefits) and the costs associated with your SEO activities.

a. Returns (Benefits)

1.   **Organic Traffic Growth**: Measure the increase in organic traffic to your website resulting from SEO efforts. This can be tracked using tools like Google Analytics.

2.   **Conversions**: Assess the number of conversions (e.g., form submissions, e-commerce transactions) that can be directly attributed to organic search traffic.

3.   **Revenue**: For e-commerce websites, calculate the revenue generated from SEO-driven conversions.

4.   **Customer Lifetime Value (CLV)**: Determine the CLV of customers acquired through organic search. CLV represents the total revenue a customer is expected to generate over their entire relationship with your business.

5.   **Brand Exposure**: Consider the value of increased brand exposure and visibility in search engine results pages (SERPs). While this is challenging to quantify precisely, it contributes to long-term brand equity.

b. Costs

1.   **SEO Expenses**: Include all costs associated with your SEO efforts, such as salaries, agency fees, content creation costs, link-building expenses, and SEO software subscriptions.

2.   **Content Creation Costs**: If you're producing content as part of your SEO strategy, account for the costs of content creation, including writing, editing, and design.

3.   **Technical SEO Expenses**: Include expenses related to technical SEO audits, website optimization, and other technical aspects.

4.   **Paid Advertising Costs**: If you're running paid search campaigns alongside SEO, separate and account for the costs of these campaigns.

3. SEO ROI Formula

The formula for calculating SEO ROI is:

ROI = (Net Profit / SEO Costs) x 100

Where:

- **Net Profit** is calculated as (Total Returns - Total Costs).

- **SEO Costs** include all expenses related to SEO efforts.

4. SEO Success Metrics

Measuring SEO success goes beyond ROI. Consider these key metrics to evaluate the effectiveness of your SEO strategies:

a. Keyword Rankings: Track improvements in keyword rankings for target keywords to assess your website's visibility in SERPs.

b. Organic Traffic Growth: Measure the increase in organic traffic over time, indicating the success of your SEO efforts in attracting visitors.

c. Click-Through Rate (CTR): Monitor improvements in CTR, particularly for high-ranking pages, as this demonstrates the effectiveness of your title tags and meta descriptions.

d. Conversion Rate: Evaluate changes in the conversion rate, indicating the ability of your SEO-optimized pages to convert visitors into leads or customers.

e. Bounce Rate: A decrease in bounce rate suggests that your SEO efforts are attracting more engaged visitors who explore your site.

f. Page Load Times: Faster page load times contribute to a positive user experience, potentially impacting SEO success.

g. Mobile Performance: Assess the impact of mobile-friendly design and mobile-first indexing on your website's performance in mobile search results.

h. Backlink Quality and Quantity: Measure improvements in the quality and quantity of backlinks, as this can positively influence search rankings.

i. Content Engagement: Track user engagement with your content, including time spent on page, social shares, and comments.

5. Attribution Models

Attribution models are essential for accurately assessing the impact of SEO on conversions. Common attribution models include:

a. Last Click Attribution: Assigns 100% of the credit for conversions to the last click or interaction before the conversion.

b. First Click Attribution: Attributes all credit to the first interaction in the conversion path.

c. Linear Attribution: Distributes credit evenly across all touchpoints in the conversion journey.

d. Time Decay Attribution: Gives more credit to interactions closer to the time of conversion.

e. Position-Based Attribution: Assigns the most credit to the first and last interactions, with the remaining credit distributed evenly among middle interactions.

6. Reporting and Communication

Effective reporting and communication of SEO ROI and success metrics are vital for aligning stakeholders and demonstrating value. Use clear, concise reports that highlight key achievements, improvements, and actionable insights. Tailor reports to the needs and preferences of different audiences, such as executives, clients, or internal teams.

7. Continuous Improvement

SEO is an ongoing process, and ROI and success metrics should be regularly reviewed and refined. Continuously optimize your strategies based on data-driven insights and evolving industry trends.

In conclusion, measuring SEO ROI and success requires a comprehensive understanding of the benefits and costs associated with your SEO efforts. By calculating ROI, tracking success metrics, using appropriate attribution models, and communicating effectively, you can demonstrate the value of SEO to your organization and make informed decisions to optimize your SEO strategy for long-term success.

Chapter 10:

SEO Trends and Future Insights

In the ever-evolving landscape of digital marketing, staying ahead of the curve is imperative for SEO professionals. As search engines, algorithms, and user behaviors continue to evolve, it's crucial to anticipate and adapt to emerging SEO trends. This chapter explores the dynamic world of SEO trends and provides valuable insights into the future of search engine optimization. We will delve into the latest developments, emerging technologies, and strategies that are shaping the SEO landscape, equipping you with the knowledge to thrive in this dynamic field.

A. Emerging SEO Technologies (AI, Machine Learning)

In the ever-evolving world of SEO, staying competitive and maintaining a strong online presence requires keeping pace with emerging technologies. Among these, artificial intelligence (AI) and machine learning (ML) are revolutionizing the way search engine optimization is practiced. In this section, we'll explore how these technologies are shaping the future of SEO and the strategies you can employ to harness their power.

1. Understanding AI and Machine Learning in SEO

a. Artificial Intelligence (AI)

AI refers to the simulation of human intelligence in computers to perform tasks that typically require human intelligence. In SEO, AI systems use algorithms and data to analyze and make informed decisions about web content, rankings, and user experience.

b. Machine Learning (ML)

Machine learning is a subset of AI that focuses on developing algorithms and models that enable systems to improve their performance through experience and data. In SEO, ML is used to enhance search algorithms, user experience, and content optimization.

2. The Role of AI and ML in SEO

a. Content Optimization and Generation

AI and ML technologies can analyze user behavior and content performance to provide insights on what type of content performs best. This includes recommendations for content length, structure, and keywords. Some AI systems can even generate content, including articles and product descriptions, with human-like quality.

b. Predictive Analytics

AI and ML can predict user behavior and search trends, helping SEO professionals anticipate shifts in demand and adjust their strategies accordingly. Predictive analytics can aid in keyword research, content planning, and campaign optimization.

c. Personalization

AI-driven personalization tailors the user experience based on individual preferences and behaviors. This includes personalized search results, content recommendations, and even website layouts. Personalization enhances user engagement and can lead to higher conversion rates.

d. Voice Search Optimization

As voice search becomes increasingly prevalent, AI and ML are used to understand natural language queries and provide more accurate and context-aware results. SEO professionals need to adapt their strategies to accommodate voice search optimization.

e. User Experience Enhancement

AI algorithms analyze user behavior and feedback to improve website usability, navigation, and overall user experience. This not only boosts SEO rankings but also leads to higher user satisfaction and retention.

f. Rank Tracking and SERP Analysis

AI-powered rank tracking tools can provide real-time insights into keyword rankings and SERP (search engine results page) changes. These tools offer competitive analysis, suggesting strategies to outrank competitors.

3. AI and ML SEO Tools

Several AI and ML-powered SEO tools and platforms are available to assist professionals in optimizing their strategies. These tools offer features like:

- **Keyword analysis and optimization suggestions**: AI algorithms can recommend the most relevant keywords, search volumes, and content optimization strategies.

- **Content generation**: Some tools can generate human-like content, allowing SEO professionals to focus on strategy and quality rather than manual content creation.

- **Natural language processing (NLP)**: NLP algorithms help in understanding user intent and crafting content that aligns with search queries.

- **Technical SEO audits**: AI-driven SEO audit tools can identify technical issues on websites, such as broken links, duplicate content, and site speed problems.

4. Ethical Considerations

As AI and ML play a more prominent role in SEO, ethical considerations become paramount. Transparency in AI decision-making, data privacy, and avoiding biases in algorithms are critical areas of concern. SEO professionals should stay informed about ethical guidelines and best practices in AI and ML implementation.

5. Preparing for the Future

To leverage emerging AI and ML technologies effectively in SEO:

• Stay updated on industry trends and advancements in AI and ML.

• Invest in AI-powered SEO tools and platforms.

• Continuously analyze and adapt your SEO strategies based on AI-driven insights.

• Emphasize user-centric optimization to align with AI's focus on enhancing user experience.

• Monitor ethical considerations and ensure compliance with data privacy regulations.

In conclusion, AI and ML are transforming the SEO landscape by providing powerful tools and strategies for optimizing websites, content, and user experiences. SEO professionals who embrace these technologies and adapt their strategies accordingly will be well-positioned to succeed in the evolving world of search engine optimization.

B. Voice Search and Conversational SEO

Voice search is rapidly changing the way people interact with search engines, and conversational SEO is emerging as a critical strategy to adapt to this shift. In this section, we'll explore the impact of voice search on SEO, the principles of conversational SEO, and strategies to optimize for voice search in the evolving digital landscape.

1. The Rise of Voice Search

Voice search is a technology that allows users to perform searches or execute commands using voice-activated devices like smartphones, smart speakers (e.g., Amazon Echo, Google Home), and virtual assistants (e.g., Siri, Google Assistant). It has gained significant popularity due to its convenience and speed.

a. Key Drivers of Voice Search

Several factors are driving the adoption of voice search:

- **Increased Use of Voice-Activated Devices**: The proliferation of smart speakers and voice-activated devices has made voice search more accessible.

- **Mobile Device Integration**: Voice assistants are integrated into mobile devices, making it easier for users to perform voice searches on the go.

- **Natural Language Processing (NLP)**: Advances in NLP technology enable voice assistants to better understand and respond to conversational queries.

2. Impact on SEO

Voice search has notable implications for SEO:

a. Longer, More Conversational Queries: Voice search queries tend to be longer and more conversational in nature compared to typed queries. Users are more likely to ask full questions, such as "What's the weather like today?" rather than typing "weather today."

b. Local SEO: Voice searches often have local intent, such as "Find a coffee shop near me." Optimizing for local SEO is crucial to appear in voice search results.

c. Featured Snippets: Voice assistants frequently read information from featured snippets (position zero) in search results. Structuring content to earn featured snippet positions is vital.

d. Mobile-Friendly Design: Voice searches are often performed on mobile devices, so having a mobile-friendly website is essential.

3. Principles of Conversational SEO

a. Natural Language Optimization: Content should be written in a conversational tone, mirroring how people speak rather than using formal, robotic language.

b. Long-Tail Keywords: Target long-tail keywords that reflect how people phrase their voice queries.

c. FAQ Pages: Create FAQ pages that answer common questions users may ask via voice search.

d. Local SEO: Optimize for local search by ensuring your business listings are accurate and up to date.

e. Schema Markup: Implement schema markup to provide structured data that voice assistants can easily understand.

f. Mobile Optimization: Ensure your website is responsive and mobile-friendly.

g. Voice Search-Friendly Content: Create content that directly answers common voice search queries.

h. User Intent: Understand user intent behind voice searches and tailor your content to address it effectively.

4. Strategies for Voice Search Optimization

a. Use of Schema Markup: Implement structured data using schema markup to provide context to search engines and voice assistants.

b. Local SEO Optimization: Claim and optimize your Google My Business listing for local voice search queries.

c. Conversational Content: Create content that addresses specific user questions and provides in-depth, conversational answers.

d. Featured Snippets: Optimize content to appear in featured snippets, as these are often read aloud in voice search results.

e. Site Speed: Ensure your website loads quickly, especially on mobile devices, to accommodate voice search users looking for fast answers.

f. Voice-Friendly Keywords: Research and target keywords that align with how people naturally speak.

g. User Experience: Prioritize user experience by making your website easy to navigate and providing clear, concise answers to voice queries.

h. Monitor Analytics: Track voice search trends in your website analytics to identify opportunities for optimization.

5. The Future of Voice Search and SEO

Voice search is continually evolving, and staying updated with industry trends is crucial. As technology advances, we can expect:

- **Improved NLP**: Voice assistants will become even better at understanding natural language, making voice search more accurate.

- **Wider Adoption**: As more devices and applications integrate voice search, it will become a standard feature.

- **Multilingual Voice Search**: Voice search will expand to accommodate multiple languages and dialects.

- **Visual Responses**: Visual responses alongside voice responses will provide users with more comprehensive information.

In conclusion, voice search is reshaping the SEO landscape, emphasizing the importance of conversational SEO. SEO professionals and businesses that adapt to these changes by optimizing for voice search queries will be better positioned to reach and engage their target audiences in an increasingly voice-activated digital world.

C. Video SEO and Visual Search

Video content and visual search are two powerful trends reshaping the way users consume information and interact with search engines. In this section, we'll delve into the significance of video SEO and the emerging field of visual search, providing insights and strategies to help you harness their potential in your digital marketing efforts.

1. Video SEO: Optimizing for Video Content

a. The Growth of Video Content

Video content has witnessed explosive growth across digital platforms, including social media, websites, and video-sharing platforms like YouTube. As users increasingly prefer video for information and entertainment, optimizing video content for search engines has become essential.

b. Key Video SEO Considerations

i. Video Hosting: Choose a reliable hosting platform for your videos, such as YouTube or Vimeo. YouTube, owned by Google, offers strong SEO integration.

ii. Video Titles and Descriptions: Craft compelling titles and detailed descriptions for your videos, incorporating relevant keywords.

iii. Thumbnails: Select attention-grabbing thumbnails that entice users to click on your videos in search results.

iv. Tags and Metadata: Use relevant tags and metadata to provide context to search engines and improve discoverability.

v. Closed Captions: Provide closed captions or subtitles to enhance accessibility and reach a broader audience.

vi. Video Sitemaps: Submit video sitemaps to search engines to help them index your video content effectively.

vii. User Engagement: Encourage user engagement with your videos through likes, shares, comments, and subscriptions, as these metrics can influence rankings.

viii. Mobile Optimization: Ensure your videos are mobile-friendly and optimized for different screen sizes.

ix. Video Schema Markup: Implement video schema markup to enhance how your video content appears in search results.

2. Visual Search: The Evolution of Search Queries

a. What Is Visual Search?

Visual search enables users to search for information using images or photographs rather than text-based queries. Users can upload an image or take a photo to find related products, information, or similar images.

b. The Role of Visual Search in SEO

Visual search is transforming how consumers discover and interact with products and services. For SEO professionals, it presents unique opportunities and challenges:

i. E-Commerce: Visual search is particularly valuable for e-commerce websites, as it allows users to find products by snapping pictures or using screenshots.

ii. Content Discovery: Visual search can help users find related content, including articles, videos, and infographics.

iii. SEO for Visual Content: To optimize for visual search, focus on image SEO, including file names, alt text, and image quality.

iv. Structured Data: Implement structured data for images to provide context to search engines and improve visibility in visual search results.

v. Mobile-Friendly Design: Given that visual searches often occur on mobile devices, ensure your website is mobile-friendly.

vi. Local SEO: Visual search can also impact local SEO, as users may seek information about businesses and landmarks using photos.

3. Strategies for Video SEO and Visual Search Optimization

a. Video SEO Strategies

i. High-Quality Content: Create engaging, informative, and high-quality video content that resonates with your target audience.

ii. Keyword Research: Conduct keyword research to identify relevant keywords and incorporate them naturally into video titles, descriptions, and tags.

iii. Video Length: Consider the optimal length for your videos, aiming to balance viewer engagement and search engine visibility.

iv. Promotion: Promote your videos through social media, email marketing, and embedding them in relevant blog posts.

v. Analytics: Monitor video performance using analytics tools to track engagement, viewer demographics, and other relevant metrics.

b. Visual Search Strategies

i. Image Optimization: Optimize images on your website by using descriptive file names and alt text that accurately represent the content.

ii. Visual Content Creation: Create visually appealing and informative content that is likely to be shared and engaged with by users.

iii. Structured Data: Implement schema markup for images to provide context to search engines and improve visual search visibility.

iv. Mobile Optimization: Ensure your website is responsive and mobile-friendly to accommodate users performing visual searches on smartphones and tablets.

v. User-Generated Content: Encourage user-generated content that includes images related to your products or services.

4. The Future of Video SEO and Visual Search

As technology continues to advance, video SEO and visual search will play increasingly significant roles in digital marketing. Expect to see innovations in AI and computer vision technologies further enhancing visual search capabilities and video recommendation algorithms.

In conclusion, video SEO and visual search are two dynamic trends that are reshaping the digital landscape. Incorporating these strategies into your SEO efforts can enhance user engagement, increase visibility in search results, and keep your digital marketing strategy aligned with evolving user preferences.

D. The Evolving Role of SEO in Digital Marketing

The role of Search Engine Optimization (SEO) in digital marketing is continually evolving, driven by changes in search engine algorithms, user behavior, and technological advancements. In this section, we will explore how SEO has transformed within the digital marketing landscape and the strategies needed to stay at the forefront of this dynamic field.

1. SEO's Integration into Digital Marketing

a. From a Standalone Practice to Integrated Strategy

In the early days of the internet, SEO was often treated as a standalone practice, primarily focused on optimizing web pages for search engines. However, it has since evolved into a fundamental component of broader digital marketing strategies. Today, successful digital marketing campaigns consider SEO from the outset, integrating it with other tactics like content marketing, social media, email marketing, and paid advertising.

b. User-Centric Approach

The evolving role of SEO emphasizes a user-centric approach. Rather than solely catering to search engines, SEO now focuses on creating valuable, informative, and engaging content that meets the needs and expectations of the target audience.

2. Content-Centric SEO

a. Content Is King

The phrase "Content is king" has become a mantra in the digital marketing world. High-quality, relevant content not only attracts visitors but also keeps them engaged, driving better search rankings and conversions. SEO professionals are now content strategists, responsible for creating, optimizing, and distributing content that resonates with the target audience.

b. Keyword Research and User Intent

Keyword research remains crucial, but it has evolved to incorporate user intent analysis. SEO professionals must understand why users are conducting specific searches and create content that not only ranks well but also satisfies those user intentions.

c. Long-Form and Multimedia Content

Long-form content, including in-depth articles, comprehensive guides, and videos, has gained prominence. These formats allow for in-depth coverage of topics, increasing the likelihood of ranking well in search results. Additionally, multimedia content, such as infographics and podcasts, contributes to a more diverse and engaging content strategy.

3. Mobile SEO and Voice Search

a. Mobile-Friendly Design

The increasing use of mobile devices for internet browsing has made mobile optimization a critical aspect of SEO. Search engines now prioritize mobile-friendly websites, and responsive design is essential to ensure a seamless user experience across devices.

b. Voice Search Optimization

Voice search has emerged as a significant trend, with more users relying on virtual assistants like Siri and Google Assistant. SEO professionals must adapt to voice search by targeting long-tail conversational keywords and optimizing content for natural language queries.

4. Local SEO and Google My Business

a. The Importance of Local Search

Local SEO has gained importance as users frequently search for nearby businesses, services, and information. Optimizing for local search involves ensuring accurate business listings, managing online reviews, and providing localized content.

b. Google My Business

Google My Business (GMB) has become a central hub for local SEO. Creating and optimizing your GMB listing, including details like business hours, address, and photos, can significantly impact local search visibility.

5. Technical SEO and Site Performance

a. Technical SEO Audits

Technical SEO remains a foundational element of SEO. Conducting regular technical audits helps identify and rectify issues like broken links, slow page load times, and crawl errors, ensuring that search engines can access and index your website effectively.

b. Core Web Vitals

Core Web Vitals, introduced by Google, focus on user experience metrics related to page loading, interactivity, and visual stability. These factors are now integrated into Google's search ranking algorithm, underscoring the importance of site performance.

6. SEO and Social Media

a. Social Signals

While social signals (e.g., likes, shares, comments) may not directly impact search rankings, they do play a role in brand visibility and user engagement. Integrating social media into your digital marketing strategy can amplify your content's reach and influence.

b. Social Listening

Social media monitoring and social listening tools allow SEO professionals to gather insights into customer sentiment, industry trends, and user-generated content. These insights can inform content creation and SEO strategies.

7. The Role of Data and Analytics

Data-driven decision-making is central to modern SEO. SEO professionals use tools like Google Analytics, SEO analytics platforms, and keyword tracking tools to monitor performance, analyze user behavior, and adjust strategies accordingly.

8. The Evolving SEO Professional

To thrive in the evolving role of SEO within digital marketing, professionals must continually update their skills. Staying current with industry trends, mastering content creation, understanding data analytics, and having a holistic view of digital marketing are all essential.

In conclusion, SEO has evolved from a standalone practice to an integral part of digital marketing strategies. It now encompasses content creation, mobile optimization, voice search, local search, technical SEO, and the integration of data analytics. Adapting to these changes is essential for SEO professionals and businesses seeking to maintain a strong online presence in the dynamic world of digital marketing.

E. Preparing for Future SEO Challenges

As the field of SEO continues to evolve, it's crucial for professionals and businesses to anticipate and prepare for future challenges. In this section, we will explore some of the potential challenges that may arise in the world of SEO and strategies to proactively address them.

1. Challenge: Evolving Search Engine Algorithms

a. Continuous Algorithm Updates

Search engines like Google frequently update their algorithms to deliver more relevant and user-friendly search results. These updates can significantly impact website rankings. Staying informed about algorithm changes and adapting SEO strategies accordingly is essential.

b. Strategy:

• Keep up-to-date with search engine guidelines and algorithm updates.

• Focus on white-hat SEO techniques that prioritize user experience and high-quality content.

- Diversify SEO strategies to reduce reliance on a single traffic source or keyword.

2. Challenge: Voice Search and Natural Language Processing

a. Voice Search Growth

The rise of voice-activated devices and virtual assistants has led to a surge in voice search. Optimizing for voice search requires understanding natural language queries and providing concise yet informative answers.

b. Strategy:

- Research and target conversational, long-tail keywords.

- Create content that directly answers common voice search queries.

- Optimize for local voice search by focusing on business listings and reviews.

3. Challenge: Mobile-First Indexing

a. Mobile Dominance

With the increasing use of smartphones for internet browsing, search engines have adopted mobile-first indexing. This means that the mobile version of your website is the primary source for ranking and indexing.

b. Strategy:

- Ensure your website is responsive and mobile-friendly.

- Prioritize mobile user experience by optimizing page speed, navigation, and content layout.

- Monitor mobile SEO performance and make adjustments as needed.

4. Challenge: Content Saturation and Quality

a. Content Overload

The internet is flooded with content, making it challenging to stand out. Quality content that provides unique value to users is more important than ever.

b. Strategy:

- Conduct thorough keyword and topic research to identify content gaps.

- Focus on creating in-depth, authoritative content that answers user questions.

- Regularly update and refresh existing content to maintain relevance.

5. Challenge: Competition and Niche Saturation

a. Increasing Competition

As more businesses recognize the importance of SEO, competition for top rankings intensifies. Niche markets may become saturated, making it harder to gain visibility.

b. Strategy:

• Differentiate your brand by offering unique products, services, or content.

• Implement local SEO strategies to target specific geographic markets.

• Invest in long-term SEO efforts that build authority and trust.

6. Challenge: Evolving User Behavior

a. Changing User Preferences

User behavior and preferences can shift over time. For example, users may increasingly rely on video content or social media for information.

b. Strategy:

• Stay attuned to changing user behavior and adapt content formats and distribution channels accordingly.

- Use analytics and user feedback to understand how visitors interact with your site.

7. Challenge: Ethical and Legal Considerations

a. Privacy and Data Protection

Increasing concerns about privacy and data protection have led to stricter regulations. SEO professionals must navigate these legal and ethical considerations.

b. Strategy:

- Ensure compliance with data protection regulations like GDPR and CCPA.

- Clearly communicate privacy policies to website visitors.

- Practice ethical link building and content creation to avoid penalties.

8. Challenge: Rapid Technological Advancements

a. Emerging Technologies

Emerging technologies like artificial intelligence (AI), augmented reality (AR), and virtual reality (VR) are changing how users interact with content and search engines.

b. Strategy:

- Stay informed about technological trends and their potential impact on SEO.

- Experiment with new technologies that align with your business goals.

- Be ready to adapt SEO strategies to accommodate emerging platforms and devices.

9. Challenge: International and Multilingual SEO

a. Global Markets

Expanding into international markets requires a comprehensive approach to SEO that considers language, cultural nuances, and regional search engines.

b. Strategy:

- Research and understand target markets, including language preferences and search habits.

- Implement hreflang tags for international SEO to indicate language and regional targeting.

- Invest in localized content and outreach strategies.

In conclusion, preparing for future SEO challenges involves staying informed, remaining adaptable, and continually refining your strategies to align with evolving search engine algorithms, user behavior, and technological advancements. By proactively addressing these challenges, SEO professionals and businesses can maintain a competitive edge in the dynamic world of digital marketing.

Chapter 11:

SEO Ethics and Best Practices

In the ever-evolving realm of Search Engine Optimization (SEO), ethical considerations and best practices are fundamental cornerstones that guide the actions of SEO professionals and digital marketers. This chapter delves into the ethical principles that underpin the practice of SEO and explores the best practices that help ensure long-term success while maintaining integrity and transparency in the digital landscape. Understanding SEO ethics is not just about compliance; it's about building trust, fostering sustainability, and creating a positive impact on the online ecosystem.

A. White Hat vs. Black Hat SEO

In the world of Search Engine Optimization (SEO), ethical considerations play a pivotal role in determining the long-term success and reputation of websites and businesses. Two distinct approaches to SEO have emerged, known as "White Hat" and "Black Hat" SEO. In this section, we will explore these two contrasting strategies, the ethical implications of each, and the importance of choosing the right path for your SEO efforts.

1. White Hat SEO

a. Definition

White Hat SEO refers to ethical and legitimate SEO practices that align with search engine guidelines and best practices. SEO professionals who follow the White Hat approach aim to improve a website's rankings in a sustainable and transparent manner.

b. Key Principles

- **Quality Content**: White Hat SEO prioritizes creating high-quality, valuable, and relevant content for users.

- **Ethical Link Building**: It focuses on acquiring backlinks through legitimate means, such as outreach and relationship-building, rather than manipulation.

- **User-Centric Optimization**: White Hat SEO aims to enhance user experience, ensuring that websites are easy to navigate, load quickly, and provide valuable information.

- **Transparency**: Practitioners of White Hat SEO are transparent about their strategies and intentions, both to search engines and users.

c. Advantages

- Long-Term Sustainability: White Hat SEO strategies are less likely to lead to penalties or search engine algorithm updates.

- Trust and Credibility: Ethical practices build trust with both search engines and users, fostering a positive online reputation.

- User Satisfaction: Prioritizing user experience leads to higher engagement, lower bounce rates, and increased conversions.

2. Black Hat SEO

a. Definition

Black Hat SEO comprises unethical and manipulative techniques aimed at exploiting search engine algorithms to achieve higher rankings quickly. These tactics often violate search engine guidelines and can lead to penalties or deindexing.

b. Key Techniques

- **Keyword Stuffing**: Overloading content with keywords to artificially boost rankings.

- **Cloaking**: Presenting different content to search engines and users to deceive search engines.

- **Link Manipulation**: Building low-quality or spammy backlinks through link farms or paid link schemes.

- **Content Scraping**: Copying and republishing content from other websites without permission.

c. Risks and Consequences

- Penalties: Black Hat SEO practices can result in search engine penalties, including ranking drops or complete removal from search results.

- Reputational Damage: Engaging in unethical SEO can harm a website's reputation, affecting trust and credibility.

- Short-Term Gains, Long-Term Losses: While Black Hat tactics may yield quick results, they are not sustainable and can lead to disastrous consequences over time.

3. Gray Hat SEO

Gray Hat SEO lies between the ethical White Hat and unethical Black Hat approaches. Practitioners of Gray Hat SEO may use tactics that push the boundaries of search engine guidelines, often exploiting loopholes or employing strategies that aren't explicitly banned.

a. Risks and Rewards

- Gray Hat strategies can yield results faster than White Hat techniques but carry a higher risk of penalties compared to ethical practices.

- The effectiveness of Gray Hat tactics can be short-lived, as search engines often catch up and update their algorithms to counter such practices.

4. The Importance of Ethical SEO

a. Trust and Credibility

Ethical SEO practices build trust with both search engines and users. A trustworthy online presence enhances brand credibility and fosters user loyalty.

b. Long-Term Sustainability

White Hat SEO strategies are more likely to withstand search engine algorithm updates and provide consistent, long-term results.

c. Reputation Management

Unethical SEO practices can tarnish a brand's reputation, resulting in a loss of trust and potential legal consequences.

d. Compliance with Guidelines

Adhering to search engine guidelines ensures that websites operate within the rules of the digital ecosystem, promoting a fair and competitive online environment.

e. User-Centric Focus

Ethical SEO prioritizes user experience, ultimately benefiting visitors to websites with relevant, valuable content.

In conclusion, the choice between White Hat, Black Hat, or Gray Hat SEO strategies is not just a matter of preference; it has a profound impact on the long-term success and ethical standing of websites and businesses in the digital landscape. While Black Hat tactics may offer short-term gains, they come with substantial risks and consequences. Ethical White Hat SEO, on the other hand, builds trust, credibility, and sustainable growth, aligning with the principles of transparency and user-centric optimization in the ever-evolving world of SEO.

B. SEO Code of Ethics

In the realm of Search Engine Optimization (SEO), ethical conduct and responsible practices are essential for maintaining trust, integrity, and credibility. To guide professionals and businesses in the ethical pursuit of SEO, various SEO organizations and experts have developed codes of ethics. In this section, we will delve into the SEO Code of Ethics, its key principles, and the importance of adhering to ethical standards in the digital landscape.

1. Definition of the SEO Code of Ethics

The SEO Code of Ethics is a set of guidelines and principles that govern the conduct of SEO professionals and organizations. It serves as a framework for ethical decision-making and responsible SEO practices. While different organizations and experts may have their own variations of the code, several common principles underpin ethical SEO:

2. Key Principles of the SEO Code of Ethics

a. Transparency

Transparency is a fundamental principle of ethical SEO. SEO professionals and businesses should provide clear and honest information about their strategies, methodologies, and intentions to both clients and website users. This includes disclosing any potential conflicts of interest.

b. Respect for Search Engine Guidelines

Ethical SEO practices align with search engine guidelines and best practices. SEO professionals should refrain from using manipulative or deceptive tactics that violate these guidelines, as such practices can lead to penalties or deindexing.

c. Quality Content Creation

Creating high-quality, valuable, and relevant content is at the core of ethical SEO. Content should be designed to meet user needs and provide genuine value, rather than being created solely for the purpose of improving rankings.

d. User-Centric Focus

Ethical SEO prioritizes the user experience. Websites should be designed for ease of navigation, fast loading times, and accessibility. Content should be engaging, informative, and organized to help users find what they need.

e. Avoiding Deceptive Practices

Ethical SEO professionals steer clear of deceptive practices such as cloaking, hidden text, keyword stuffing, and link schemes. These tactics not only violate search engine guidelines but also undermine user trust.

f. Ethical Link Building

Link building is a crucial aspect of SEO, but ethical practitioners focus on building high-quality, relevant, and authoritative backlinks. They avoid spammy or manipulative link-building practices.

g. Continuous Education and Adaptation

Staying informed about the latest SEO trends, technologies, and algorithm updates is vital. Ethical SEO professionals engage in ongoing education and adapt their strategies to align with evolving best practices.

3. Importance of Adhering to the SEO Code of Ethics

a. Trust and Credibility

Adhering to ethical standards builds trust with both clients and website users. Trust is a cornerstone of successful online businesses and brand reputation.

b. Long-Term Sustainability

Ethical SEO strategies are more likely to withstand search engine algorithm updates and provide consistent, long-term results. Unethical practices can lead to penalties and ranking drops.

c. Compliance with Legal and Regulatory Standards

Ethical SEO practices ensure compliance with legal and regulatory standards, such as data protection and copyright laws. This minimizes legal risks and potential liabilities.

d. Competitive Advantage

Businesses that adhere to ethical SEO practices have a competitive advantage in the online marketplace. Users are more likely to engage with and trust websites that follow ethical guidelines.

e. Positive User Experience

Ethical SEO prioritizes user-centric optimization, resulting in a positive user experience. This, in turn, leads to higher user engagement, lower bounce rates, and increased conversions.

4. Certification and Industry Associations

Many SEO professionals seek certification from industry associations that uphold ethical standards. These associations often have their own codes of ethics and offer certification programs to validate professionals' adherence to ethical SEO practices.

Conclusion

The SEO Code of Ethics serves as a compass for SEO professionals and businesses, guiding them toward ethical decision-making and responsible practices in the dynamic digital landscape. Adhering to these principles not only fosters trust, credibility, and sustainability but also ensures compliance with legal standards and promotes a positive user experience—a testament to the commitment of ethical SEO professionals to the principles of transparency, integrity, and user-centric optimization.

C. Avoiding Penalties and Algorithmic Updates

Search engine algorithms are constantly evolving to improve the quality of search results and provide users with the most relevant and valuable content. To maintain a strong online presence and ethical SEO practices, it's crucial to understand how to avoid penalties and navigate algorithmic updates effectively. In this section, we'll explore the strategies and best practices for avoiding penalties and adapting to algorithmic changes.

1. Understanding Search Engine Penalties

a. What Are Penalties?

Search engine penalties are punitive actions taken by search engines like Google to penalize websites that violate their guidelines. Penalties can result in lower search rankings, decreased visibility, or even removal from search results altogether.

b. Common Causes of Penalties

Some common reasons websites may incur penalties include:

- **Unethical SEO Practices**: Engaging in Black Hat or Gray Hat SEO tactics, such as keyword stuffing, cloaking, or buying links, can trigger penalties.

- **Duplicate Content**: Publishing duplicate or

plagiarized content can lead to penalties.

- **Low-Quality Backlinks**: Having a high number of spammy or irrelevant backlinks pointing to your site can result in penalties.

- **User Experience Issues**: Slow page load times, poor mobile optimization, and inaccessible content can lead to penalties.

c. Impact of Penalties

Penalties can have severe consequences, including:

- Reduced organic search traffic.

- Loss of credibility and trust with users.

- Damage to brand reputation.

- Potential loss of revenue and business opportunities.

2. Avoiding Penalties through Ethical SEO

a. Prioritize White Hat SEO

Adhering to White Hat SEO principles, which emphasize ethical and user-centric practices, is the best way to avoid penalties. Focus on quality content, ethical link building, and transparent strategies.

b. Regular Audits and Compliance Checks

Conduct regular SEO audits to identify and rectify potential issues that could trigger penalties. Ensure compliance with search engine guidelines and best practices.

c. High-Quality Content

Create original, informative, and engaging content that satisfies user intent. Avoid duplicate content, keyword stuffing, and content scraping.

d. Link Quality and Diversity

Build high-quality, relevant backlinks through ethical outreach and relationship-building. Avoid low-quality and spammy link schemes.

e. Mobile Optimization

Optimize your website for mobile devices to provide a seamless user experience. Google prioritizes mobile-friendly websites.

f. Page Speed and Technical SEO

Address technical SEO issues, such as slow page load times, broken links, and crawl errors. Core Web Vitals, which measure user experience factors, have become a crucial ranking factor.

3. Navigating Algorithmic Updates

a. Understanding Algorithmic Updates

Search engines like Google frequently update their algorithms to improve search results. These updates can significantly impact website rankings. Stay informed about major algorithm changes and their potential effects on your website.

b. Recovery from Algorithmic Changes

If your website is negatively affected by an algorithmic update, take the following steps:

• Analyze the changes: Understand how the update has affected your website's performance.

• Identify issues: Determine if there are specific issues, such as content quality or technical problems, that need addressing.

• Make improvements: Take corrective actions based on your analysis to align your website with the new algorithm's requirements.

• Monitor results: Continuously monitor your website's performance to assess the impact of your changes and make further adjustments if necessary.

c. Diversify SEO Strategies

Avoid overreliance on a single SEO strategy or tactic. Diversify your approach to reduce vulnerability to algorithmic changes. This might include exploring different content formats, outreach methods, and marketing channels.

d. Stay Informed

Stay updated on industry news, algorithmic changes, and best practices by following reputable SEO blogs, forums, and official announcements from search engines.

4. The Ongoing Journey of SEO

SEO is an ongoing process that requires vigilance and adaptability. Avoiding penalties and navigating algorithmic updates is a continual effort that necessitates ethical practices, monitoring, and a commitment to delivering value to users.

In conclusion, avoiding penalties and adapting to algorithmic updates are essential components of ethical SEO practices. By prioritizing White Hat SEO, staying informed about algorithm changes, and maintaining a user-centric approach, you can build and sustain a strong online presence while navigating the ever-changing landscape of search engine optimization.

D. Ethical Link Building and Content Creation

Link building and content creation are two cornerstones of effective SEO, but they must be approached with ethics and integrity to maintain trust and credibility in the digital landscape. In this section, we will delve into ethical practices for link building and content creation, emphasizing how these strategies contribute to a sustainable and reputable online presence.

1. Ethical Link Building

a. Definition

Link building is the process of acquiring high-quality, relevant backlinks to your website from other reputable websites. Ethical link building involves obtaining backlinks through legitimate means and adhering to search engine guidelines.

b. Principles of Ethical Link Building

• **Quality over Quantity**: Prioritize high-quality backlinks over a large quantity of low-quality links. One authoritative, relevant link can carry more weight than multiple irrelevant ones.

• **Relevance**: Seek backlinks from websites that are relevant to your industry or niche. Relevance enhances the value of the link in the eyes of search engines.

- **Transparency**: Be transparent about your intentions when seeking backlinks. Clear communication and ethical outreach are key.

- **Natural Link Growth**: Avoid manipulative practices like buying links or participating in link schemes. Instead, focus on natural link growth through valuable content and relationship-building.

- **Diversity**: Aim for a diverse link profile that includes different types of links, such as guest posts, mentions, and citations, from a variety of sources.

c. Ethical Link Building Strategies

- **Guest Blogging**: Contribute high-quality guest posts to reputable websites in your niche. Ensure that your guest posts provide value to the readers.

- **Outreach and Relationship-Building**: Build relationships with industry influencers, bloggers, and website owners. Ethical outreach can lead to organic backlink opportunities.

- **Content Collaboration**: Collaborate with others in your industry on content projects, such as ebooks, webinars, or research studies. Shared content can naturally result in backlinks.

- **Public Relations**: Share noteworthy achievements,

events, or company news to attract media coverage and earn organic mentions and backlinks.

2. Ethical Content Creation

a. Definition

Content creation involves producing informative, valuable, and relevant content for your website's audience. Ethical content creation focuses on providing genuine value and avoiding deceptive or manipulative practices.

b. Principles of Ethical Content Creation

- **User-Centric**: Prioritize content that serves the needs and interests of your audience. User-centric content is more likely to engage and satisfy visitors.

- **Originality**: Create original content that is not copied or plagiarized. Avoid duplicating content from other sources.

- **Accuracy**: Ensure that the information presented in your content is accurate and fact-checked. Misleading or false information can harm trust and credibility.

- **Relevance**: Keep your content relevant to your target audience and industry. Avoid "clickbait" or misleading headlines that promise information not delivered in the content.

- **Transparency**: Clearly disclose any affiliations,

sponsorships, or conflicts of interest within your content, especially if you promote products or services.

c. Ethical Content Creation Strategies

- **Research and Citations**: Support your content with credible sources, research studies, and citations. Give credit where it's due and acknowledge the work of others.

- **Original Insights**: Offer unique insights, perspectives, or analyses that distinguish your content from others in your industry.

- **Engagement and Interaction**: Encourage user engagement by inviting comments, questions, and discussions. Ethical content fosters a sense of community and participation.

- **Accessibility**: Ensure that your content is accessible to all users, including those with disabilities. This includes providing alternative text for images and using accessible design practices.

- **Privacy and Data Protection**: Respect user privacy and adhere to data protection regulations when collecting and handling user information.

3. The Ethical SEO Ecosystem

Ethical link building and content creation are integral parts of an ethical SEO ecosystem. They contribute to:

- **Trust and Credibility**: Ethical practices build trust with users and search engines, fostering credibility and loyalty.

- **Long-Term Sustainability**: Ethical strategies are more likely to withstand algorithm updates and provide consistent, long-term results.

- **User Satisfaction**: Prioritizing user needs and interests leads to higher user engagement and satisfaction.

- **Brand Reputation**: Ethical practices enhance brand reputation and image, making it a valuable asset in the digital landscape.

In conclusion, ethical link building and content creation are not only best practices but also essential components of responsible SEO. By adhering to ethical guidelines, focusing on user value, and maintaining transparency and integrity, you can build a sustainable and reputable online presence that benefits both your audience and your business.

E. Section: Sustainable and Long-Term SEO Strategies

Sustainability and longevity are paramount considerations when developing an effective SEO strategy. Sustainable SEO strategies not only help maintain and improve search engine rankings over time but also contribute to ethical and responsible digital practices. In this section, we will explore the principles and techniques behind sustainable and long-term SEO strategies.

1. Understanding Sustainable SEO

a. Definition

Sustainable SEO refers to the practice of implementing strategies and tactics that endure and adapt to changes in search engine algorithms, user behavior, and industry trends. These strategies are designed to provide lasting value to both users and search engines.

b. Key Principles of Sustainable SEO

- **Ethical Practices**: Sustainable SEO is built on ethical and white-hat practices that comply with search engine guidelines. Ethical practices foster trust and credibility.

- **User-Centric Focus**: A user-centric approach prioritizes creating content and experiences that meet the needs and expectations of the target audience.

- **Adaptability**: Sustainable SEO strategies are adaptable and flexible, allowing for adjustments in response to algorithmic changes and evolving user behavior.

- **Quality Content**: High-quality, valuable, and relevant content is at the core of sustainability. Content should provide long-term value to users.

- **Diverse Traffic Sources**: Relying on a variety of traffic sources, such as organic search, social media, email marketing, and referral traffic, reduces dependency on a single channel.

- **Ongoing Measurement and Analysis**: Regularly monitoring performance metrics and conducting data analysis help identify areas for improvement and optimization.

2. Techniques for Sustainable SEO

a. Content Strategy

- **Evergreen Content**: Create evergreen content that remains relevant and valuable to users over time. This content continues to attract organic traffic and backlinks.

- **Content Updates**: Regularly update and refresh existing content to ensure accuracy and relevance. Google rewards fresh and up-to-date content.

- **Cornerstone Content**: Develop cornerstone content that serves as a comprehensive resource on a specific topic or theme. It can attract sustained traffic and backlinks.

b. Ethical Link Building

- **Relationship Building**: Invest in relationships with

industry influencers, bloggers, and website owners for organic and ethical backlink opportunities.

- **Guest Blogging**: Contribute high-quality guest posts to reputable websites within your niche, focusing on providing value to readers.

- **Link Earning**: Focus on creating valuable content that naturally earns backlinks. User-centric content attracts organic mentions and citations.

c. Technical SEO

- **Mobile Optimization**: Ensure your website is mobile-friendly and optimized for mobile users. Google's mobile-first indexing prioritizes mobile-optimized websites.

- **Site Speed**: Optimize page load times and website performance to provide a smooth user experience. Fast-loading websites are favored by both users and search engines.

- **Structured Data**: Implement structured data (schema markup) to enhance search engine understanding of your content and improve visibility in rich snippets.

d. Social Signals and Engagement

- **Social Media Engagement**: Maintain an active presence on social media platforms to engage with your audience and drive traffic to your website.

- **User Interaction**: Encourage user interaction on your website, such as comments, reviews, and discussions, to enhance user engagement and signal content value.

e. Regular Monitoring and Adaptation

- **Algorithm Updates**: Stay informed about search engine algorithm updates and adapt your strategies accordingly. Analyze the impact of updates on your website and make necessary adjustments.

- **Performance Metrics**: Continuously monitor key performance metrics, including organic traffic, rankings, conversions, and user behavior. Use data-driven insights to refine your strategy.

3. Benefits of Sustainable SEO

- **Longevity**: Sustainable SEO strategies are built to withstand the test of time and adapt to changes, ensuring your online presence remains strong over the long term.

- **Credibility and Trust**: Ethical and user-centric practices build credibility and trust with both search engines and users, enhancing your brand's reputation.

- **Consistent Traffic**: Sustainable strategies lead to

consistent organic traffic, reducing the risk of drastic ranking fluctuations.

- **Reduced Dependency**: Diverse traffic sources reduce reliance on organic search alone, mitigating the impact of potential algorithmic changes.

4. Conclusion

Sustainable and long-term SEO strategies are essential for building a strong and enduring online presence. By focusing on ethical practices, user-centric content, adaptability, and ongoing measurement, businesses and SEO professionals can navigate the ever-evolving digital landscape while providing lasting value to their audiences. Sustainable SEO is not just a short-term tactic; it's a commitment to responsible and ethical digital marketing practices that stand the test of time.

Chapter 12:

Case Studies and Practical Applications

In the world of Search Engine Optimization (SEO), theory and principles come to life through real-world examples and practical applications. This chapter is dedicated to the exploration of case studies that showcase successful SEO campaigns, practical insights into overcoming challenges, and industry-specific strategies. By delving into these case studies and practical applications, readers can bridge the gap between theory and implementation, gaining valuable insights into how SEO strategies translate into tangible results across diverse contexts and industries.

A. Real-World Examples of Successful SEO Campaigns

In the dynamic landscape of SEO, real-world examples of successful campaigns serve as invaluable sources of inspiration and education. They provide concrete evidence of the impact of SEO strategies and tactics, demonstrating how businesses and websites have achieved remarkable results through effective optimization efforts. In this section, we will delve into several real-world examples of successful SEO campaigns, highlighting key strategies and takeaways.

1. Moz's Whiteboard Friday

Moz, a well-known authority in the field of SEO, has been running a successful SEO campaign called *Whiteboard Friday*. This ongoing video series features in-depth explanations of various SEO concepts and strategies. The success of Whiteboard Friday can be attributed to the following factors:

- **High-Quality Content**: Each video provides valuable insights and actionable advice on SEO topics, making it a go-to resource for SEO professionals and enthusiasts.

- **Consistency**: Moz consistently releases new episodes every Friday, building a loyal audience that anticipates and values their content.

- **Engagement**: Viewers are encouraged to ask questions and engage with the content, fostering a sense of community and ongoing interaction.

Takeaway: Consistently producing high-quality, educational content can position a brand as an industry leader and attract a dedicated following.

2. Dollar Shave Club

Dollar Shave Club, a subscription-based grooming products

company, achieved remarkable SEO success through a combination of content marketing and clever SEO tactics. They created an engaging and humorous promotional video that went viral, attracting millions of views and backlinks from authoritative websites. Key elements of their success include:

- **Viral Content**: The viral video not only increased brand awareness but also generated natural backlinks and social media mentions.

- **User-Centric Approach**: The video resonated with their target audience, leading to a surge in organic traffic and subscriptions.

- **Link Earning**: By creating shareable content, Dollar Shave Club earned high-quality backlinks naturally.

Takeaway: Creative, shareable content that aligns with your audience's interests can lead to organic backlinks and significant traffic growth.

3. Airbnb's Neighborhood Guides

Airbnb leveraged local SEO and content marketing to create neighborhood guides for various cities. These guides provide travelers with insights into different neighborhoods, highlighting local attractions and accommodations. The success factors include:

- **Local SEO Optimization**: Optimizing content for local search keywords allowed Airbnb to rank prominently in local search results.

- **User Value**: The guides provide valuable information to users, enhancing their experience on the platform and increasing user engagement.

- **Long-Tail Keywords**: The guides target long-tail keywords related to specific neighborhoods, attracting highly relevant organic traffic.

Takeaway: Focusing on local SEO and providing valuable, location-specific content can drive traffic, improve user experience, and boost engagement.

4. HubSpot's Blog

HubSpot, a marketing software company, has built a thriving blog that serves as a cornerstone of its content marketing strategy. By consistently producing informative and educational blog posts, HubSpot has achieved the following:

- **Traffic Growth**: The blog attracts millions of monthly visitors, driving organic traffic to the website.

- **Lead Generation**: Valuable content encourages readers to subscribe, providing a steady stream of leads for HubSpot's products.

- **Authority Building**: The blog's extensive library of content establishes HubSpot as a thought leader in the marketing and sales industry.

Takeaway: A well-maintained blog with informative content can drive organic traffic, generate leads, and position a brand as an industry authority.

Conclusion

These real-world examples of successful SEO campaigns underscore the diverse strategies and approaches that can lead to impressive results. Whether through educational content, viral marketing, local SEO, or blogging, businesses and organizations can achieve their goals by applying effective SEO principles and practices to their unique contexts. The key is to understand the audience, create valuable content, and stay committed to ethical and user-centric SEO strategies.

B. SEO Challenges and Solutions

Search Engine Optimization (SEO) is a dynamic and ever-evolving field, and with its growth come various challenges that website owners, marketers, and SEO professionals must navigate. This section explores common SEO challenges and provides practical solutions to address them effectively.

Mastering Search Engine Optimization (SEO)

1. Challenge: Google Algorithm Updates

Solution: Stay Informed and Adapt

Google frequently updates its search algorithms to improve user experience and combat spammy tactics. These updates can significantly impact website rankings. To address this challenge:

- **Stay Informed**: Follow reputable SEO news sources and Google's official announcements to keep up with algorithm changes.

- **Continuous Monitoring**: Regularly monitor your website's performance and rankings, especially after major updates. Be prepared to adapt your strategy if needed.

- **Focus on Quality**: Emphasize high-quality content, user experience, and ethical SEO practices. These elements are less likely to be adversely affected by algorithm updates.

2. Challenge: Competitive SEO Landscape

Solution: Differentiate and Optimize

Competition for search rankings is fierce, especially in popular niches. To stand out:

- **Keyword Research**: Target long-tail keywords and niche-specific terms to capture a more engaged audience.

- **Unique Content**: Create original and valuable content that sets your website apart from competitors.

- **Link Building**: Build high-quality, relevant backlinks through ethical outreach and relationship-building.

3. Challenge: Mobile Optimization

Solution: Prioritize Mobile-Friendly Design

With mobile users accounting for a significant portion of web traffic, mobile optimization is essential:

- **Responsive Design**: Ensure your website is responsive and adapts to various screen sizes and devices.

- **Mobile Page Speed**: Optimize page load times for mobile users to provide a smooth experience.

- **Mobile-First Indexing**: Understand Google's mobile-first indexing and ensure your website complies.

4. Challenge: Content Quality and Relevance

Solution: Focus on User-Centric Content

Content is at the heart of SEO success. To improve content quality and relevance:

- **Audience Research**: Understand your target audience's needs, interests, and pain points.

- **Keyword Optimization**: Use keywords naturally within content to align with user intent.

- **Regular Updates**: Keep content fresh and up-to-date to maintain relevance.

5. Challenge: Technical SEO Issues

Solution: Technical Audit and Optimization

Technical SEO issues, such as broken links, crawl errors, and site speed problems, can hinder rankings:

- **Technical Audit**: Conduct regular audits to identify and fix technical issues.

- **Structured Data**: Implement structured data (schema markup) to enhance search engine understanding.

- **Website Speed**: Optimize page load times and server response times.

6. Challenge: Backlink Profile Quality

Solution: Ethical Link Building

A strong backlink profile is essential, but it must consist of high-quality, relevant links:

- **Quality over Quantity**: Prioritize high-authority, niche-specific backlinks over a large number of low-quality links.

- **Outreach**: Build relationships with industry influencers and website owners for organic backlink opportunities.

7. Challenge: Local SEO Competitiveness

Solution: Local SEO Strategies

Local SEO can be highly competitive. To improve local rankings:

- **Google My Business**: Optimize your Google My Business listing with accurate information, images, and reviews.

- **Local Citations**: Ensure consistency of your business's name, address, and phone number (NAP) across online directories.

- **Customer Reviews**: Encourage and manage customer reviews, which play a role in local rankings.

8. Challenge: User Experience (UX)

Solution: Enhance Website UX

User experience is a ranking factor and influences user behavior:

- **Website Speed**: Optimize for fast loading times.

- **Mobile Optimization**: Ensure a seamless experience

on mobile devices.

- **Navigation and Accessibility**: Simplify navigation and make content accessible.

9. Challenge: International SEO

Solution: International SEO Strategies

Expanding internationally requires thoughtful SEO strategies:

- **Hreflang Tags**: Implement hreflang tags to indicate language and regional targeting.

- **Localized Content**: Create content tailored to specific regions and languages.

- **Cultural Considerations**: Understand cultural nuances that may impact content and messaging.

Conclusion

SEO challenges are inherent in the digital landscape, but they can be overcome with a combination of knowledge, strategy, and adaptability. By staying informed, focusing on user-centric practices, and continuously monitoring and optimizing your website, you can navigate these challenges and achieve sustainable SEO success.

C. Industry-Specific SEO Strategies

Effective SEO strategies often require customization to suit the unique characteristics and challenges of specific industries. In this section, we will explore industry-specific SEO strategies, delving into key considerations, tactics, and best practices for various sectors.

1. E-Commerce SEO Strategies

a. Key Considerations

E-commerce websites face fierce competition and must optimize for product pages, user experience, and conversions.

b. Tactics and Best Practices

- **Optimize Product Pages**: Use descriptive titles, high-quality images, and detailed product descriptions with relevant keywords.

- **User Experience**: Ensure seamless navigation, fast load times, and a secure checkout process to reduce bounce rates and improve conversions.

- **Content Marketing**: Create informative blog posts, guides, and videos to educate users and drive organic traffic.

- **Product Reviews**: Encourage and display user-generated product reviews to build trust and credibility.

2. Local Business SEO Strategies

a. Key Considerations

Local businesses aim to attract customers in specific geographic areas and need to focus on local search optimization.

b. Tactics and Best Practices

- **Google My Business**: Optimize your Google My Business listing with accurate information, images, and reviews.

- **Local Citations**: Ensure consistency of your business's name, address, and phone number (NAP) across online directories.

- **Customer Reviews**: Encourage and manage customer reviews, which play a role in local rankings.

- **Local Content**: Create content related to local events, news, and community engagement to connect with the local audience.

3. Healthcare SEO Strategies

a. Key Considerations

The healthcare industry has specific regulations and requires trust-building through authoritative content.

b. Tactics and Best Practices

- **HIPAA Compliance**: Ensure compliance with the Health Insurance Portability and Accountability Act (HIPAA) when handling patient data.

- **Authoritative Content**: Publish accurate and well-researched medical content authored by experts to build trust.

- **Local SEO**: Target local search terms to attract patients in specific regions.

- **Mobile Optimization**: Optimize for mobile users, as many patients use smartphones to search for healthcare information.

4. Legal SEO Strategies

a. Key Considerations

Law firms face competition for legal keywords and must establish authority and trust.

b. Tactics and Best Practices

- **Keyword Selection**: Target long-tail keywords and niche-specific terms related to legal specialties.

- **Content Marketing**: Create comprehensive legal guides, blog posts, and case studies to showcase expertise.

- **Local SEO**: Optimize for local search to attract clients in specific regions.

- **Link Building**: Build high-quality backlinks from legal directories, authoritative legal websites, and local listings.

5. Travel and Hospitality SEO Strategies

a. Key Considerations

Travel and hospitality websites rely on enticing visuals and persuasive content to attract travelers.

b. Tactics and Best Practices

- **Visual Content**: Use high-quality images, videos, and virtual tours to showcase destinations and accommodations.

- **Content Marketing**: Create travel guides, itineraries, and destination-focused content to engage and inform travelers.

- **User Reviews**: Encourage and display user-generated reviews to build trust.

- **Mobile Optimization**: Optimize for mobile users, as travelers often research and book on mobile devices.

6. Tech and Software SEO Strategies

a. Key Considerations

Tech and software companies operate in highly competitive spaces and need to demonstrate expertise and innovation.

b. Tactics and Best Practices

• **Keyword Research**: Target keywords related to software solutions, features, and industry trends.

• **Educational Content**: Produce whitepapers, case studies, and technical documentation to showcase expertise.

• **Content Updates**: Keep software documentation and resources up-to-date to maintain relevance.

• **Backlink Building**: Secure high-quality backlinks from tech blogs and industry publications.

7. Nonprofit SEO Strategies

a. Key Considerations

Nonprofits aim to raise awareness, attract donors, and engage supporters through their online presence.

b. Tactics and Best Practices

• **Storytelling**: Share compelling stories and narratives to connect with donors and supporters emotionally.

- **Transparency**: Clearly communicate the organization's mission, goals, and financial transparency.

- **Local SEO**: Optimize for local search to attract local supporters and volunteers.

- **Content Marketing**: Publish informative content related to the nonprofit's cause and impact.

Conclusion

Industry-specific SEO strategies require a deep understanding of the unique challenges and objectives within each sector. By tailoring SEO tactics to align with the needs of the industry, businesses and organizations can effectively reach their target audience, build authority, and achieve their goals in the digital landscape. Whether it's optimizing e-commerce product pages, engaging local customers, or establishing authority in the healthcare field, industry-specific strategies are key to SEO success.

D. SEO in E-Commerce, Local Business, and Content Websites

Search Engine Optimization (SEO) strategies vary significantly depending on the type of website and its goals. In this section, we will delve into the unique SEO challenges and strategies for three distinct types of websites: E-Commerce, Local Business, and Content Websites.

1. SEO for E-Commerce Websites

a. Key Challenges

E-commerce websites face fierce competition, an extensive product catalog, and the need to drive conversions.

b. SEO Strategies

- **Product Page Optimization**: Optimize individual product pages with descriptive titles, high-quality images, and detailed descriptions.

- **Keyword Research**: Target product-specific keywords and long-tail keywords to capture user intent.

- **User Experience (UX)**: Ensure seamless navigation, fast page load times, and an intuitive checkout process to reduce bounce rates and improve conversions.

- **Content Marketing**: Create blog posts, guides, and videos to educate users, showcase products, and drive organic traffic.

- **Structured Data**: Implement schema markup to enhance search engine understanding of product details, prices, and availability.

2. SEO for Local Businesses

a. Key Challenges

Local businesses rely on attracting customers within specific geographic areas and face the challenge of local search optimization.

b. SEO Strategies

• **Google My Business (GMB) Optimization**: Optimize your GMB listing with accurate information, images, and customer reviews.

• **Local Citations**: Ensure consistency of your business's name, address, and phone number (NAP) across online directories.

• **Local Content**: Create content related to local events, news, and community engagement to connect with the local audience.

• **Customer Reviews**: Encourage and manage customer reviews, which play a significant role in local rankings.

• **Local Link Building**: Build local backlinks from authoritative local websites, directories, and organizations.

3. SEO for Content Websites

a. Key Challenges

Content websites, including blogs and news outlets, need to consistently produce high-quality, engaging content to attract and retain readers.

b. SEO Strategies

- **Keyword Research**: Identify relevant keywords and topics to target with your content. Use tools to find high-volume, low-competition keywords.

- **Content Quality**: Prioritize well-researched, informative, and engaging content that addresses user needs and interests.

- **On-Page Optimization**: Optimize meta titles, descriptions, and headings for SEO. Ensure a clear content structure.

- **Content Promotion**: Share content on social media, through email marketing, and in relevant online communities to increase visibility and attract readers.

- **Internal Linking**: Create a logical internal linking structure to guide readers to related content and improve user experience.

- **Backlinks**: Attract backlinks from authoritative websites by creating valuable and shareable content.

4. Common SEO Strategies Across All Types of Websites

While each type of website has its unique challenges and strategies, some common SEO practices are universally applicable:

- **Mobile Optimization**: Ensure that websites are mobile-friendly, as mobile users make up a significant portion of web traffic.

- **User Experience (UX)**: Create a seamless and user-friendly experience through intuitive navigation, fast page load times, and easy access to information.

- **Technical SEO**: Regularly audit websites for technical issues such as broken links, crawl errors, and duplicate content.

- **Monitoring and Analytics**: Use tools like Google Analytics to monitor key performance metrics, track user behavior, and make data-driven decisions.

- **Ethical and White-Hat SEO**: Adhere to ethical SEO practices, such as avoiding black-hat tactics, duplicate content, and link schemes, to build a reputable online presence.

Conclusion

SEO strategies vary significantly based on the type of website and its specific goals and challenges. E-commerce websites focus on product optimization and conversions, local businesses prioritize local search visibility and customer reviews, and content websites emphasize high-quality, engaging content and reader engagement. While the tactics differ, the core principles of mobile optimization, user experience, technical SEO, monitoring, and ethical practices remain essential for SEO success across all types of websites. Understanding these nuances is crucial for website owners and SEO professionals seeking to achieve their goals in the digital landscape.

E. Learning from SEO Success Stories

SEO success stories provide valuable insights into effective strategies, best practices, and the transformative power of search engine optimization. In this section, we will explore the importance of studying and learning from these success stories and how they can inspire and inform your own SEO efforts.

1. Gaining Inspiration and Motivation

SEO success stories often highlight remarkable achievements, such as dramatic traffic growth, increased rankings, and substantial revenue gains. These stories can inspire and motivate

SEO professionals, website owners, and marketers to aim for similar results.

2. Understanding Diverse Strategies

Success stories come from various industries and niches, showcasing a wide range of SEO strategies and tactics. By studying these stories, you can gain a deeper understanding of the diversity of approaches that lead to success. This knowledge can help you tailor your SEO strategy to your specific goals and industry.

3. Identifying Key Takeaways

Successful SEO campaigns often share common elements and best practices. By dissecting these stories, you can identify key takeaways that apply to your own SEO efforts. Some common takeaways include:

- **Quality Content**: Many success stories emphasize the importance of high-quality, informative, and engaging content. This reaffirms that content is a cornerstone of SEO.

- **Ethical Practices**: Success stories often showcase websites that adhere to ethical and white-hat SEO practices. Avoiding black-hat tactics is essential for long-term success.

- **User-Centric Approach**: User experience and user-centric design are frequently mentioned as factors contributing to

SEO success. Prioritizing user needs and expectations is crucial.

- **Adaptability**: Some success stories involve websites that adapt to changing search engine algorithms and user behavior. Flexibility and adaptability are key.

- **Link Building**: Building high-quality backlinks from authoritative sources is a common theme in many success stories. Link building remains a critical SEO strategy.

4. Learning from Mistakes

Success stories don't always paint a perfect picture. Some stories may also include challenges and mistakes made along the way. These insights into failures and setbacks can be just as valuable as success stories. They provide opportunities to learn from others' experiences and avoid common pitfalls.

5. Staying Updated

SEO is an ever-evolving field, and what worked in the past may not work as effectively today. Success stories often reflect the SEO landscape at the time of their success. Therefore, it's essential to stay updated with the latest SEO trends and algorithm changes to ensure your strategies remain effective.

6. Case Study Analysis

To effectively learn from SEO success stories, consider

conducting a case study analysis. Break down the success story into key components, including goals, strategies, tactics, challenges, and results. This structured analysis can provide actionable insights for your own SEO campaigns.

7. Conclusion

SEO success stories are more than just tales of triumph; they are valuable educational resources. By studying these stories, you can gain inspiration, identify best practices, learn from mistakes, and adapt strategies to your unique goals and industry. Whether you're optimizing a website, launching a new campaign, or seeking continuous improvement, success stories can be powerful tools for informed decision-making and achieving SEO success.

Conclusion

As we draw the final curtain on this journey through these pages, we invite you to reflect on the knowledge, insights, and discoveries that have unfolded before you. Our exploration of various subjects has been a captivating voyage into the depths of understanding.

In these chapters, we have ventured through the intricacies of numerous topics and examined the key concepts and findings that define these fields. It is our hope that you have found inspiration, enlightenment, and valuable takeaways that resonate with you on your own quest for knowledge.

Remember that the pursuit of understanding is an ever-evolving journey, and this book is but a milestone along the way. The world of knowledge is vast and boundless, offering endless opportunities for exploration and growth.

As you conclude this book, we encourage you to carry forward the torch of curiosity and continue your exploration of these subjects. Seek out new perspectives, engage in meaningful discussions, and embrace the thrill of lifelong learning.

We express our sincere gratitude for joining us on this intellectual adventure. Your curiosity and dedication to expanding your horizons are the driving forces behind our shared quest for wisdom and insight.

Thank you for entrusting us with a portion of your intellectual journey. May your pursuit of knowledge lead you to new heights and inspire others to embark on their own quests for understanding.

With profound gratitude,

Nikhilesh Mishra, Author

Recap of Key

As you've journeyed through the comprehensive guide, "Mastering Search Engine Optimization: Concepts, Techniques, and Applications," it's essential to pause and recap the key SEO principles and techniques you've encountered. This section serves as a valuable summary and a reminder of the core takeaways from your exploration of SEO.

1. Understanding SEO's Core Principles:

- **User-Centric Approach**: SEO revolves around providing the best possible user experience. Prioritizing user needs and expectations is foundational.

- **Content Quality**: High-quality, relevant, and informative content is at the heart of SEO. Content should resonate with your target audience and address their queries.

- **Keyword Research**: Keyword research is the foundation of SEO strategy. It involves identifying the terms and phrases your audience uses to search for information.

- **Technical SEO**: Technical aspects such as website speed, mobile-friendliness, and structured data (schema markup) are crucial for SEO success.

- **Link Building**: Building authoritative and high-quality backlinks remains a vital element of SEO. It's about earning trust from other reputable websites.

2. On-Page Optimization:

- **Title Tags, Meta Descriptions, Headers**: Crafting compelling and keyword-rich title tags, meta descriptions, and headers can improve click-through rates and rankings.

- **Content Quality, Relevance, and Length**: High-quality content should be relevant to the user's intent and sufficiently detailed to answer their questions.

- **Image SEO and Alt Text**: Optimizing images with descriptive alt text enhances accessibility and SEO.

- **URL Structure and Internal Linking**: Creating clean and descriptive URLs, along with strategic internal linking, enhances both user experience and SEO.

- **Mobile-Friendly Design**: Mobile-friendliness and responsive design are essential for reaching users on various devices.

3. Off-Page SEO:

- **Backlinks and Link Building Strategies**: Earning backlinks from authoritative sources remains a cornerstone of off-page SEO.

- **Social Media Signals**: Social media engagement can indirectly influence SEO through increased visibility and traffic.

- **Online Reputation Management**: Maintaining a positive online reputation is vital for trust and credibility.

- **Guest Blogging and Influencer Outreach**: Collaborating with influencers and guest posting can expand your online presence.

- **Content Marketing**: High-quality content can naturally attract backlinks and social signals.

4. Technical SEO:

- **Website Speed**: Faster-loading websites provide a better user experience and may rank higher.

- **XML Sitemaps and Robots.txt**: These tools help search engines crawl and index your site effectively.

- **Canonicalization and Duplicate Content**: Avoiding duplicate content issues is crucial for SEO.

- **Schema Markup and Rich Snippets**: Structured data can enhance how your content appears in search results.

- **HTTPS and Security**: Secure websites are favored by search engines and users.

5. Local SEO:

- **Google My Business Optimization**: Optimizing your Google My Business listing is essential for local visibility.

- **Local Citations and NAP Consistency**: Consistency in name, address, and phone number listings across the web is vital.

- **Customer Reviews and Ratings**: Positive reviews can boost local rankings and trust.

6. Mobile SEO:

- **Mobile-Friendly Design**: Responsive and mobile-friendly websites are crucial for mobile SEO.

- **Mobile Page Speed**: Faster-loading mobile pages improve user experience.

- **Accelerated Mobile Pages (AMP)**: Implementing AMP can enhance mobile performance and visibility.

7. SEO Analytics and Reporting:

- **Setting Up Google Analytics**: Accurate tracking of SEO performance is essential.

- **SEO Performance Metrics**: Monitoring traffic, rankings, and conversions provides insights into your SEO strategy's effectiveness.

- **SEO Reporting Tools and Dashboards**: Tools can simplify the process of tracking and reporting on SEO metrics.

- **A/B Testing and Experimentation**: Experimentation helps optimize your SEO strategy over time.

- **SEO ROI and Measuring Success**: Understanding the return on investment (ROI) of your SEO efforts is crucial.

8. SEO Trends and Future Insights:

- **Emerging SEO Technologies**: Keep an eye on emerging technologies like AI and machine learning in SEO.

- **Voice Search and Conversational SEO**: The rise of voice search is changing the way users interact with search engines.

- **Video SEO and Visual Search**: Visual content is becoming increasingly important in SEO.

- **The Evolving Role of SEO in Digital Marketing**: SEO is integral to the broader digital marketing landscape.

- **Preparing for Future SEO Challenges**: Stay adaptable and informed to tackle the challenges of an ever-evolving SEO landscape.

By recapping these key principles and techniques, you solidify your understanding of SEO and its multifaceted aspects. As you move forward in your journey as an SEO practitioner, remember that mastering SEO is an ongoing pursuit, and staying informed about industry trends and evolving technologies is essential.

Thank you for joining us on this insightful exploration of SEO, and we wish you continued success in your SEO endeavors.

With profound gratitude,

Nikhilesh Mishra, Author

The Ongoing Journey of Mastering SEO

As you conclude your journey through "Mastering Search Engine Optimization: Concepts, Techniques, and Applications," it's crucial to understand that mastering SEO is not a destination but an ongoing and dynamic journey. SEO is an ever-evolving field that requires continuous learning, adaptation, and refinement. This section delves into the concept of the ongoing journey of mastering SEO.

1. The Ever-Changing Landscape of SEO:

- **Algorithm Updates**: Search engines like Google frequently update their algorithms to provide more accurate and relevant search results. SEO practitioners must stay informed about these updates and adjust their strategies accordingly.

- **Emerging Technologies**: The integration of artificial intelligence (AI) and machine learning in search algorithms is reshaping how search engines rank and display content. SEO professionals need to adapt to these technological advancements.

- **User Behavior**: User behavior and expectations are constantly evolving. SEO specialists must monitor user trends and adjust their strategies to meet changing user needs.

2. Staying Informed and Educated:

- **SEO Communities**: Joining SEO communities, forums, and social media groups can provide valuable insights into industry trends and best practices. Engaging with peers allows for knowledge sharing and networking.

- **Continual Learning**: Invest in ongoing education and training. SEO professionals should attend conferences, workshops, and webinars to stay updated on the latest techniques and technologies.

- **Reading Industry Publications**: Regularly reading SEO-related publications, blogs, and news sources helps practitioners stay informed about industry developments.

3. The Importance of Testing and Experimentation:

- **A/B Testing**: Experimentation with A/B testing allows SEO practitioners to assess the impact of changes to their websites and content. It helps in fine-tuning strategies for better results.

- **Data-Driven Decision-Making**: Making decisions based on data and analytics is central to SEO success. Regularly analyzing performance metrics and user behavior data guides ongoing optimization efforts.

4. Ethical Considerations:

- **White Hat SEO**: Staying ethical in SEO practices is not only a best practice but also crucial for long-term success. Avoiding unethical practices like keyword stuffing or link schemes is essential.

- **User Experience**: Prioritizing the user experience is an ongoing commitment. SEO professionals should continually enhance website usability, load times, and mobile-friendliness.

- **Content Quality**: Consistently delivering high-quality, relevant content that meets user needs and expectations is a long-term strategy for SEO success.

5. Adaptation to Industry-Specific Trends:

- **Industry-Specific SEO**: Different industries may have unique SEO challenges and trends. Staying attuned to industry-specific SEO practices and developments is vital for success.

- **Local SEO**: For businesses with a local presence, staying current with local SEO trends, such as Google My Business updates, is crucial.

6. Collaboration and Communication:

- **Interdisciplinary Collaboration**: SEO is often intertwined with other digital marketing disciplines. Effective collaboration with teams handling content, social media, and web development ensures a holistic approach to SEO.

- **Client Communication**: SEO professionals working with clients should maintain open and transparent communication, explaining strategies, results, and ongoing improvements.

7. Preparing for Future Challenges:

- **Anticipating Algorithmic Changes**: SEO practitioners should develop strategies to mitigate potential negative impacts of algorithmic updates and capitalize on new opportunities.

- **Voice Search and Mobile-First Indexing**: As voice search and mobile-first indexing continue to evolve, SEO specialists should focus on optimizing for these trends.

- **International SEO**: Expanding into global markets may require adapting SEO strategies for different languages and regions.

In essence, mastering SEO is a dynamic journey that requires adaptability, a commitment to ethical practices, and a dedication to ongoing education. SEO professionals must embrace change, stay informed about industry developments, and continuously refine their strategies to remain competitive in the ever-evolving landscape of search engine optimization.

As you conclude this book, remember that your journey in mastering SEO is just beginning. Embrace the challenges, stay curious, and never stop learning as you navigate the ever-changing terrain of SEO.

With profound gratitude,

Nikhilesh Mishra, Author

Glossary of Terms

In the ever-evolving world of SEO, understanding the terminology is akin to speaking the language of search engine optimization fluently. This glossary serves as a valuable reference guide, providing in-depth explanations of key SEO terms and concepts you've encountered throughout this book.

1. Algorithm: A set of rules or calculations that search engines use to determine the order in which search results are displayed. Search engines like Google use complex algorithms to rank web pages.

2. Backlink: A link from one website to another. High-quality backlinks from authoritative websites can improve a site's search engine ranking.

3. Canonicalization: A process used to consolidate multiple URLs that lead to the same content into a single, preferred URL. This helps prevent duplicate content issues.

4. CTR (Click-Through Rate): The percentage of users who click on a specific link or ad after seeing it. In SEO, CTR is often used to measure the effectiveness of title tags and meta descriptions.

5. Keywords: Specific words or phrases that users type into search engines to find information. Keyword research is essential for SEO to identify which terms to target.

6. Long-Tail Keywords: Longer and more specific keyword phrases that usually have lower search volume but can attract highly targeted traffic.

7. Meta Description: A brief summary of a web page's content that appears in search engine results. It should be enticing and informative to encourage clicks.

8. NAP (Name, Address, Phone Number): Consistency in the way a business's name, address, and phone number are listed across the web is crucial for local SEO.

9. Page Speed: The time it takes for a web page to load completely. Faster-loading pages tend to rank higher in search results and provide a better user experience.

10. SERP (Search Engine Results Page): The page displayed by a search engine in response to a user's query. It typically includes organic (unpaid) and paid search results.

11. Schema Markup: A type of structured data that can be added to web pages to provide search engines with more detailed information about the content. It can result in rich snippets in search results.

12. Title Tag: An HTML element that specifies the title of a web page. It appears in search engine results as the clickable link.

13. User Intent: The primary goal or purpose of a user's online search. Understanding user intent is essential for creating content that meets their needs.

14. Voice Search: A technology that allows users to perform searches by speaking their queries aloud rather than typing them. Voice search optimization is becoming increasingly important.

15. White Hat SEO: Ethical SEO practices that align with search engine guidelines. White hat SEO focuses on creating high-quality content and building genuine, organic backlinks.

16. XML Sitemap: A file that lists all the pages on a website and provides information about their structure. It helps search engines crawl and index a site more effectively.

17. 404 Error: A standard HTTP response code indicating that the web page the user requested could not be found. Properly handling 404 errors is important for user experience and SEO.

This glossary offers a glimpse into the terminology used in the field of SEO. As you continue your journey in mastering search engine optimization, referencing this glossary will help you navigate the complex world of SEO terms and concepts with confidence. Remember that SEO is a multifaceted discipline, and staying informed about its terminology is key to success.

Resources and References

As you reach the final pages of this book by Nikhilesh Mishra, consider it not an ending but a stepping stone. The pursuit of knowledge is an unending journey, and the world of information is boundless.

Discover a World Beyond These Pages

We extend a warm invitation to explore a realm of boundless learning and discovery through our dedicated online platform: **www.nikhileshmishra.com**. Here, you will unearth a carefully curated trove of resources and references to empower your quest for wisdom.

Unleash the Potential of Your Mind

- **Digital Libraries:** Immerse yourself in vast digital libraries, granting access to books, research papers, and academic treasures.

- **Interactive Courses:** Engage with interactive courses and lectures from world-renowned institutions, nurturing your thirst for knowledge.

- **Enlightening Talks:** Be captivated by enlightening talks delivered by visionaries and experts from diverse fields.

- **Community Connections:** Connect with a global community of like-minded seekers, engage in meaningful discussions, and share your knowledge journey.

Your Journey Has Just Begun

Your journey as a seeker of knowledge need not end here. Our website awaits your exploration, offering a gateway to an infinite universe of insights and references tailored to ignite your intellectual curiosity.

Acknowledgments

As I stand at this pivotal juncture, reflecting upon the completion of this monumental work, I am overwhelmed with profound gratitude for the exceptional individuals who have been instrumental in shaping this remarkable journey.

In Loving Memory

To my father, **Late Shri Krishna Gopal Mishra,** whose legacy of wisdom and strength continues to illuminate my path, even in his physical absence, I offer my deepest respect and heartfelt appreciation.

The Pillars of Support

My mother, **Mrs. Vijay Kanti Mishra,** embodies unwavering resilience and grace. Your steadfast support and unwavering faith in my pursuits have been the bedrock of my journey.

To my beloved wife, **Mrs. Anshika Mishra,** your unshakable belief in my abilities has been an eternal wellspring of motivation. Your constant encouragement has propelled me to reach new heights.

My daughter, **Miss Aarvi Mishra,** infuses my life with boundless joy and unbridled inspiration. Your insatiable curiosity serves as a constant reminder of the limitless power of exploration and discovery.

Brothers in Arms

To my younger brothers, **Mr. Ashutosh Mishra** and **Mr. Devashish Mishra,** who have steadfastly stood by my side, offering unwavering support and shared experiences that underscore the strength of familial bonds.

A Journey Shared

This book is a testament to the countless hours of dedication and effort that have gone into its creation. I am immensely grateful for the privilege of sharing my knowledge and insights with a global audience.

Readers, My Companions

To all the readers who embark on this intellectual journey alongside me, your curiosity and unquenchable thirst for knowledge inspire me to continually push the boundaries of understanding in the realm of cloud computing.

With profound appreciation and sincere gratitude,

Nikhilesh Mishra

September 17, 2023

About the Author

Nikhilesh Mishra is an extraordinary visionary, propelled by an insatiable curiosity and an unyielding passion for innovation. With a relentless commitment to exploring the boundaries of knowledge and technology, Nikhilesh has embarked on an exceptional journey to unravel the intricate complexities of our world.

Hailing from the vibrant and diverse landscape of India, Nikhilesh's pursuit of knowledge has driven him to plunge deep into the world of discovery and understanding from a remarkably young age. His unwavering determination and quest for innovation have not only cemented his position as a thought leader but have also earned him global recognition in the ever-evolving realm of technology and human understanding.

Over the years, Nikhilesh has not only mastered the art of translating complex concepts into accessible insights but has also crafted a unique talent for inspiring others to explore the limitless possibilities of human potential.

Nikhilesh's journey transcends the mere boundaries of expertise; it is a transformative odyssey that challenges conventional wisdom and redefines the essence of exploration. His commitment to pushing the boundaries and reimagining the norm serves as a luminous beacon of inspiration to all those who aspire to make a profound impact in the world of knowledge.

301

Mastering Search Engine Optimization (SEO)

As you navigate the intricate corridors of human understanding and innovation, you will not only gain insight into Nikhilesh's expertise but also experience his unwavering dedication to empowering readers like you. Prepare to be enthralled as he seamlessly melds intricate insights with real-world applications, igniting the flames of curiosity and innovation within each reader.

Nikhilesh Mishra's work extends beyond the realm of authorship; it is a reflection of his steadfast commitment to shaping the future of knowledge and exploration. It is an embodiment of his boundless dedication to disseminating wisdom for the betterment of individuals worldwide.

Prepare to be inspired, enlightened, and empowered as you embark on this transformative journey alongside Nikhilesh Mishra. Your understanding of the world will be forever enriched, and your passion for exploration and innovation will reach new heights under his expert guidance.

Sincerely, **A Fellow Explorer**

Notes

Notes

Notes

Notes

Notes

Notes

Notes

Notes